T0032159

"Thanks to the painstaki[ng]
Campbell—by hand, while [...]
the anglophone world i[...]
this concise yet crucial te[xt...]
interlocking and conflicting revolutionary traditions,
Revolutionary Affinities is a welcome invitation to find each
other, through our rejection of all forms of oppression,
with every tool available to us—a convergent lens of
Marxism and anarchism provides invaluable vision."
—Natasha Lennard, author of *Being
Numerous: Essays on Non-Fascist Life*

"David Campbell's highly accessible translation sheds
new light on the deep, complex relationship between the
revolutionary labor movement's two ideological drivers—
Marxists and anarchists—during a moment in which
understanding that history could not be more essential.
It is a timely effort to illuminate our bloody, brilliant,
shared history, and to inspire today's revolutionaries
to keep pushing forward in the struggle, together."
—Kim Kelly, journalist and author of *Fight Like
Hell: The Untold History of American Labor*

"Michael Löwy is unquestionably a tremendous figure
in the decades-long attempt to recover an authentic
revolutionary tradition from the wreckage of Stalinism."
—Dominic Alexander, *Counterfire*

"To say that exchanges between anarchists and Marxists have not always been cordial would be euphemistic. Yet, anticapitalist libertarians and libertarian Marxists have a lot in common as this brief account by two libertarian Marxists demonstrates, offering a historical panorama of the relations between the two currents and a comradely contribution to their debate."
—Gilbert Achcar, author of many books, including *Perilous Power* (coauthored with Noam Chomsky) and *Morbid Symptoms*

KAIROS

In ancient Greek philosophy, *kairos* signifies the right time or the "moment of transition." We believe that we live in such a transitional period. The most important task of social science in time of transformation is to transform itself into a force of liberation. Kairos, an editorial imprint of the Anthropology and Social Change department housed in the California Institute of Integral Studies, publishes groundbreaking works in critical social sciences, including anthropology, sociology, geography, theory of education, political ecology, political theory, and history.

Series editor: Andrej Grubačić

Recent and featured Kairos books:

Zapatista Stories for Dreaming An-Other World by Subcomandante Marcos

We Are the Crisis of Capital: A John Holloway Reader by John Holloway

In, Against, and Beyond Capitalism: The San Francisco Lectures by John Holloway

Practical Utopia: Strategies for a Desirable Society by Michael Albert

A New World in Our Hearts: Noam Chomsky in Conversation with Michael Albert

Autonomy Is in Our Hearts: Zapatista Autonomous Government through the Lens of the Tsotsil Language by Dylan Eldredge Fitzwater

Building Free Life: Dialogues with Öcalan edited by International Initiative

The Art of Freedom: A Brief History of the Kurdish Liberation Struggle by Havin Guneser

The Sociology of Freedom: Manifesto of the Democratic Civilization, Volume III by Abdullah Öcalan

The Battle for the Mountain of the Kurds: Self-Determination and Ethnic Cleansing in the Afrin Region of Rojava by Thomas Schmidinger

For more information visit www.pmpress.org/blog/kairos/

Revolutionary Affinities
Toward a Marxist-Anarchist Solidarity

Michael Löwy and Olivier Besancenot

Translated by David Campbell

Revolutionary Affinities: Toward a Marxist-Anarchist Solidarity
Michael Löwy and Olivier Besancenot
Originally published as *Affinités révolutionnaires: Nos étoiles rouges et noires: Pour une solidarité entre marxistes et libertaires* by Éditions Mille Et Une Nuits © 2014
Translated by David Campbell
This edition © 2023 PM Press

ISBN: 978-1-62963-969-7 (paperback)
ISBN: 978-1-62963-984-0 (ebook)
Library of Congress Control Number: 2022931964

Cover design by John Yates/www.stealworks.com
Interior design by briandesign

10 9 8 7 6 5 4 3 2 1

PM Press
PO Box 23912
Oakland, CA 94623
www.pmpress.org

Printed in the USA

Contents

I Points of Solidarity

Portraits

II Points of Conflict

III A Few Libertarian Marxist Thinkers

IV Policy Issues

In memory of Clément Méric

Preface to the English Language Edition

Since the 2014 publication of this book in France, there have been several new manifestations of the revolutionary affinities between Marxists and anarchists. In this short introduction we can only mention a few examples.

One of the most impressive is the revolutionary experience in Rojava, a majority-Kurdish region in northwestern Syria where a liberation movement has tried, since 2012, to establish an autonomous power inspired by the libertarian socialism of Murray Bookchin and the democratic confederalism of Abdullah Öcalan, the founder of the Kurdistan Workers' Party. The leading force of the process is the Democratic Union Party, a Kurdish movement linked to the Kurdistan Workers' Party, in alliance with Arab communities hostile to Daesh, as well as several other ethnic or religious communities (Yezidis, Assyrians, Armenians, etc.). It is a unique experience that rejects nationalism, the nation-state, and capitalist patriarchy, and tries to promote a democratic administration rooted in local assemblies. The self-emancipation of women—which led, among other initiatives, to the creation of the Women's Protection Units, a female armed body—is one of the most essential components of the Rojava Revolution. It is also a fragile experiment that had to fight for its survival against the murderous armies of Daesh and is currently threatened by the semifascist Turkish regime of Erdogan.

Marxists and anarchists have been active together in the international solidarity movements with Rojava. More importantly, activists of both persuasions were among the hundreds of volunteers who have come—inspired by the example of the International Brigades in Spain from 1936 to 1939—from many countries, including Canada, France, Germany, Italy, Spain, the United States, and the United Kingdom, to fight in the ranks of the People's Protection Units and the Women's Protection Units, against Daesh first and the Turkish intervention afterward. Marxists and anarchists, men and women, were among those who gave their lives to defend the Rojava revolutionary project. In this case, the revolutionary affinity became a brotherhood and sisterhood in blood.

All international volunteers take Kurdish pseudonyms. "Dilsoz," an Italian activist, explained his reasons for joining the fight in Rojava: "I'm an anarcho-communist. This revolution is built upon libertarian ideas. Revolutions are the heritage of all of humanity.... The women's armed units are the spectacular demonstration that, for the first time in thousands of years in this region, men and women are equal."

All volunteers, once they arrive in Rojava, are also asked to record a video to be made public in the event of their death in action. Here are the words left by "Tekoşer," the Kurdish name of the Italian fighter Lorenzo Orsetti: "I have no regrets. I died doing what I believed was right, defending the weak and staying true to my ideals of justice, equality, and freedom. Always remember that 'every storm begins with a single raindrop.' And try to be that raindrop yourself."

Without taking such a dramatic form, struggles uniting Marxists and anarchists have been taking place in many countries, including the United States. A striking example in the US is the coming together of both traditions in the antifascist movement, confronting the sinister development of altright, racist, fascist, and neo-Nazi groups. The terrible Trump years encouraged this alliance, either in the form of formal

coalitions, such as Outlive Them NYC, or simply in joint participation in actions. David Campbell, the translator of this book
(and an anarcho-communist) produced this English translation
in jail: he had been sentenced to eighteen months for his participation in an open confrontation of Marxist and anarchist
antifascists with so-called alt-right Trump supporters in New
York in 2018.

France is another country where such common initiatives have taken place during the last few years—in numerous
demonstrations against police violence, in trade-union struggles, and in popular semi-insurrectionary movements such
as the Yellow Vests. Another important field of unified action
here, like in the US, is the antifascist movement against the
National Front (the Le Pen family party, since 2018 rebranded
the National Rally) and other, smaller, neofascist groups. This
book is dedicated to the memory of Clément Méric, a young
antifascist activist who belonged to the Confédération nationale du travail (National Confederation of Labor), an anarcho-
syndicalist union, and to Action antifasciste Paris-Banlieue.
In June 2013, Méric was killed in a street confrontation with
a fascist gang, the Jeunesses nationalistes révolutionnaires
(Revolutionary Nationalist Youth), which has since been
outlawed. Every year in June, his memory is celebrated in a
common demonstration by French antifascists, both Marxist
and anarchist.

Similar examples could be given from many other countries: Greece, Germany, the United Kingdom, and several in
Latin America.

We hope this book will be a modest contribution to the
alliance between the black and red banners in the English-
speaking world.

Olivier Besancenot and Michael Löwy

Translator's Acknowledgments

I translated this book by hand, in jail on Rikers Island, with the help of a gigantic 1,500-page unabridged Larousse French dictionary. I was very fortunate before, during, and after my incarceration, to be the recipient of constant, earnest, and responsive support from a dedicated group of friends, family, and others, including many total strangers, from across the country and around the world. At every step along the way, people showed more support than I ever could have imagined, including in the process of translating this book. It was essentially a long dialogue via the United States Postal Service: I would first translate a section of the book, writing every word, footnote, and punctuation mark by hand. Then I would mail it to the group of friends (mostly anarchists, and a few Marxists) who had agreed to help me with this project. They, in turn, would scan my handwritten translations, page by page, into a shared folder, where they were then organized and painstakingly typed and formatted only to be printed and mailed back to me. I'd mark them up with a second round of edits and mail them back for the group to scan and tinker with again. There were also several people who took it on themselves to answer my questions about the French text—researching historical and theoretical context and particularly difficult terms, typing their findings and explanations up in spreadsheets, which were also printed out and mailed to me. In retrospect, I'm kind of amazed it worked.

It wasn't until after my release that I was able to actually finish the translation for a number of reasons. But the vast bulk of this work was done in the manner described above, and though I've been searching for words to express my gratitude since I began, I still haven't managed to find them. The best I can do is offer my deepest and most sincere thanks to those who helped me make it happen. Without their support, this translation would have been absolutely impossible. More than anything, I am grateful for the stranger in Kansas City who took the initiative and sent me that French dictionary. In no particular order, then, those without whom the English version of this book would definitely not exist:

Stephen Campbell
Victor Malaret
Carmichael Monaco
Liz Ciavolino
Christopher Hoffman
Andrew Hamm
Robert Wood Lynn
Kim Kelly
Dylan Baron
Maura McCreight
Natasha Lennard
Benoît Pereira
Liz Geist
Jarrod Shanahan
Michelle Miller
Katie Yow
Stevie
Tonia
The David Campbell Defense Committee
Ramsey Kanaan and PM Press
The kind stranger in Kansas City, Missouri

Translator's Note

When I began translating this book from French to English, a few fragments had already been translated by Michael Löwy. Some of these fragments have been incorporated into my translation, or have informed it in some way.

I have left all of the authors' original footnotes intact and added my own footnotes, in brackets, for historical or cultural context where appropriate.

Note on the Use of the Term *Libertaire*

In one of these fragments, Löwy explains his use of the French word *libertaire* in the English translation: "I use the French term," he writes, "which refers to a broad antiauthoritarian *revolutionary socialist* tendency, because its English equivalent, 'libertarian,' has been hijacked by an ultra-liberal *capitalist reactionary* ideology."

The term *libertaire* was first used by French anarcho-communist Joseph Déjacque in 1857 to describe his own politics as antiauthoritarian, but deeply left-wing (i.e., egalitarian and progressive). In France and throughout most of the world, this is still the meaning attached to the word.

In the 1960s, a capitalist American political scientist and economist named Murray Rothbard began successfully co-opting the term's English equivalent, *libertarian*, to describe a political stance that was skeptical of authority, but otherwise right-wing (i.e., capitalist and antisocial). This usage is now by far the most common usage of the term *libertarian* in the United States.

Anarchists and others who are skeptical of authority but whose politics are otherwise egalitarian or progressive are sometimes described in English as "left-libertarians" (as opposed to right-libertarians); there are also *autonomists* (usually Marxists or anarchists), who prioritize local autonomy and decision-making, and *antiauthoritarians*, a broad term denoting anyone opposed to an excess of authority. None of these, however, quite captures the original meaning of *libertaire*. With this in mind, I have chosen to follow Löwy's lead, and retain the use of the term from the original French. Technically, *libertaire* is a broader term than *anarchist*, and describes anyone, anarchist or not, who is skeptical of authority, and while anarchists could be said to fit within the libertaire tradition, not all libertaires favor the complete abolition of the state, as anarchists do. Generally speaking, however, *anarchist* and *libertaire* can be thought of as interchangeable for the purposes of this book.

One exception: when *libertaire* precedes a noun like *Marxist* or *communist*, I have translated it as *libertarian*. This is common practice in English as it should be clear to readers that the ideology discussed is left-wing in character. Hence, "libertarian communism," etc.

Foreword

The histories of the labor movement recount in detail the disagreements, conflicts, and confrontations between Marxists and anarchists. The partisans of the two currents have not been shy about composing theoretical or historical works that denounce their adversaries' depravity. Some have even made it their specialty to carry out this moral "execution" of the other. An illustrious example, and a telling one, is the title of one of Joseph Stalin's first books, *Anarchism or Socialism?* (1907). The future secretary of the Communist Party of the Soviet Union wrote: "We believe that the Anarchists are real enemies of Marxism. Accordingly, we also hold that a real struggle must be waged against real enemies."[1] We know what comes next....

The objective of our book is exactly the opposite. It is undertaken in the spirit of the First International—2014 was the 150th anniversary of its founding (September 28, 1864)—a pluralistic revolutionary association that saw, at least in its early years, significant convergences between the two currents of the radical Left. Another side of history exists, no less important, but often forgotten and sometimes even deliberately obscured: that of the alliances and active solidarity between anarchists and Marxists. This story is long, though little known for more than a century and even still today. Certainly, we do not underestimate the conflicts, particularly the bloody Kronstadt confrontation (1921), to which we devote an entire chapter. But fraternity in a common struggle has nonetheless existed since the Paris Commune. Testifying to it are those great historical figures, from Louise Michel to Subcomandante Marcos, who have attracted the attention and sympathy of Marxists as well as libertaires (anarchists, anti-authoritarians, etc.), and those thinkers who have embodied a libertarian Marxist sympathy, such as Walter Benjamin, André Breton, and Daniel Guérin. A number of questions have always been points of contention between socialism and anarchism, have always divided Marxists and libertaires; it is no longer so much a question of "settling the debate" as it is of making use of these reflections to find leads for possible new convergences. The questions posed here are not designed to be exhaustive. We have chosen to discuss "taking power," eco-socialism, economic planning, federalism, direct democracy, and the union-party relationship.

Our hope is that *the future will be red and black*; the anti-capitalism, the socialism, or the communism of the twenty-first century will need to draw from both these sources of radicalism. We want to sow a few seeds of libertarian Marxism in the hope that they will find fertile ground to grow, and bear leaves and fruit.

PS: We shared the writing of the chapters between us—each of us has his own style and approach—but we discussed their contents, which express our common ideas. Two of the texts, more personal, are signed: the letter to Louise Michel (Olivier Besancenot) and the section on Benjamin Péret (Michael Löwy).

I

Points of Solidarity

The First International and the Paris Commune (1871)

London, 1871. The International Workingmen's Association (IWA)—known today as the First International—was founded more than 150 years ago, in 1864, at Saint Martin's Hall in London by a European workers' congress which had been convened by the English unions. The newly elected general council charged Karl Marx with writing its Inaugural Address, the founding speech and document of the modern workers' movement. The IWA's general rules begin with the famous declaration, "The emancipation of the working classes must be conquered by the working classes themselves."

From the beginning, anarchists and libertaires,[1] most notably Proudhonians, were present in the First International, and their relations with the Marxian socialists were not strictly antagonistic. Between the supporters of Marx and the representatives of the left-Proudhonian current, such as Eugène Varlin and his friends, there was considerable agreement. Both opposed the right-Proudhonians, supporters of "mutualism"—an economic system based upon "equal exchange" between small proprietors. At the Brussels Congress of the First International in 1868, the alliance between the two leftist tendencies resulted in the adoption—under the guidance of the Belgian libertaire militant César de Paepe—of a "collectivist" program. This resolution proposed making collective property of the means of production: the lands, forests, mines, machines, and means of transportation.[2] The resolution on the forests appears, retrospectively, as one of the most interesting ones, for its *social and ecological* significance: "Considering that the abandonment of forests to private individuals causes the destruction of woods necessary for the conservation of springs, and, as a matter of course, of the good qualities of the soil, as well as the health and lives of the population, the Congress thinks that the forests ought to remain the property of society."[3]

After Mikhail Bakunin joined the First International in 1868, and the success of the libertaires' proposals at the Congress of Basel in 1869, the tensions with Marx and his followers intensified. However, during the Paris Commune in 1871 the two currents worked closely together, in the first great attempt at a proletarian power in modern history. Already in 1870, Leo Frankel, a Hungarian labor activist established in France (and a close friend of Marx), and Eugène Varlin, the dissident Proudhonian, had been working together for the reorganization of the French section of the IWA. After March 18, 1871, both were at the head of the Paris Commune, the former as delegate for labor and exchange, the latter as delegate for war, working in close cooperation. Both took part, in May 1871, in the fight against the Versailles forces; Varlin was executed by firing squad after the defeat of the Commune, while Frankel was able to escape and emigrate to London.[4]

Despite its short-lived nature—only a few months—the Commune of 1871 is an unparalleled case in the history of social revolutions. It was the first historical example of a revolutionary workers' power, democratically organized—delegates were elected by universal suffrage—and doing away with the bureaucratic apparatus of the bourgeois state. It was also a profoundly *pluralistic* experience, bringing together in one struggle "Marxists" (the term didn't exist yet), left-Proudhonians, Jacobins, Blanquists, and social republicans. The Commune inspired most of the great revolutionary movements of the twentieth century, but its democratic-revolutionary and pluralistic qualities would be much less present in the movements that succeeded it, save at the very beginning of the October Revolution of 1917.

Of course, Marx's and Bakunin's respective analyses of the Commune were diametrically opposed. One could summarize Marx's interpretation by the following quote: "The small group of convinced socialists who participated in the Commune were in a very difficult position.... They had to set up a revolutionary government and army against the government and army of Versailles."

Against this understanding of the civil war in France, as between two governments and two armies, Bakunin presented a strong antistatist viewpoint: "[The Paris Commune] was a Revolution against the *State* itself, of this supernaturalist abortion of society."

Attentive and well-informed readers will have already corrected these misattributions: the first opinion is that of Bakunin himself, as presented in his essay "The Paris Commune and the Idea of the State,"[5] and the second is a quote by Marx in his first draft of *The Civil War in France*.[6] We inverted the statements on purpose to show that the (undeniably real) divergences between Marx and Bakunin, Marxists and anarchists, are not as simple and obvious as one might believe.

In any case, Marx rejoiced in the fact that, over the course of the Commune, the Proudhonians had forgotten the teachings of their master, while some libertaires observed with pleasure that Marx's writings on the Commune overlooked centralism in favor of federalism. Indeed, *The Civil War in France*, which Marx hurriedly dashed off at the request of the IWA, and the drafts and preparatory materials for his book, bear witness to Marx's fervent antistatism. In it, he defines the Commune as "the political form of the social emancipation of the workers," "at last discovered," and insisted that it was a rupture with the state, which he refers to variously as an "artificial body," "boa constrictor," "deadening incubus," and "parasitical excrescence."[7]

After the Commune, however, the conflict between the two socialist tendencies worsened, coming to a head at the Congress of the Hague in 1872, with the expulsion of Bakunin and his Swiss follower James Guillaume and the moving of the seat of the IWA to New York, which was essentially its dissolution. Following this split, the libertaires decided to form their own International Workingmen's Association, which still exists in some sense today; it serves as a link between anarchist movements in various countries.

Instead of tallying up each other's errors and wrongs—there has been no shortage of insults or accusations—we would rather put forward the most positive aspect of this experiment: a diverse, democratic, multifaceted internationalist movement in which distinct political opinions were able to come together in thought and in action for several years—a feat that allowed these alliances, both short- and long-lived, to play a leading role in the first great modern proletarian revolution, an international where anarchists and Marxists were able to work together and take action together, despite their conflicts. It was, of course, an experiment that cannot be repeated, but that still interests us today, at the dawn of the twenty-first century.

The Second International, founded in 1889, was from the outset dominated by the Marxist faction. Anarchist tendencies were nonetheless present until the Congress of Zurich in 1893, which saw the expulsion of Gustav Landauer and the German libertaires, soon followed by a split. Among the dissidents who broke away from the Zurich Congress were not only anarchists such as Fernand Pelloutier, but also antiparliamentary socialists, such as the Dutch Ferdinand Domela Nieuwenhuis and the French Jean Allemane.

May Day and the Haymarket Martyrs (1886)

Chicago, 1886. As we know—or rather, as we *should* know, living as we do in a culture that encourages us to forget—the history of May Day begins in Chicago in 1886. The American unions had called for a general strike to demand the eight-hour day—at that time, workers had to labor for ten, twelve, or fourteen hours a day. The strike started on May 1, 1886, and in the following days it spread and intensified. On May 3, in front of the McCormick factory, the police fired on the crowd, killing four workers. The following day, the trade-union Left—predominantly anarcho-syndicalist—called for a protest against the police's actions at Haymarket Square. When the police ordered the protesters to disperse, someone—it has never been determined who—threw a bomb at the police, killing eight of them and wounding sixty. In response, the police fired into the crowd, killing an unknown number and wounding two hundred.

Unable to find the person responsible for throwing the bomb, the authorities arrested the eight principal leaders of the revolutionary syndicalist movement in the city, who had organized the protest, and subjected them to a parody of justice. Condemned for their beliefs, their radical publications, and their revolutionary calls to join the struggle, most of them got the death penalty. One of them, Louis Lingg, committed suicide with dynamite; the other four (August Spies, Albert

Figure 1. Portraits of the martyrs of Chicago: (1) Samuel Fielden, (2) Albert Parsons, (3) Louis Lingg, (4) August Spies, (5) Michael Schwab, (6) Adolph Fischer, and (7) George Engel. (Illustration adapted from *Frank Leslie's Illustrated Newspaper*, November 12, 1887.)

Parsons, Adolph Fischer, and George Engel) were hanged on November 11, 1887. On the scaffold, noose around his neck, Spies spoke his last words, which would be engraved in bronze letters on the monument to the Haymarket Martyrs: "There will be a time when our silence will be more powerful than the voices you strangle today." A few years later in 1893, the newly elected Governor of Illinois, John P. Altgeld, pardoned the murdered activists, recognizing that most of the "evidence" brought by the prosecution during the trial had been "a pure fabrication."[1]

Who were these libertaire fighters of Chicago, pioneers in the struggle for the eight-hour day, and victims of the class-based justice system, like Sacco and Vanzetti a few decades later?

August Spies was a German immigrant who had discovered socialist ideas in America. An activist with the Socialist Labor Party, he had even run for office as the party's candidate. He was the editor of the German-language newspaper *Arbeiter-Zeitung* (Workers' journal). Beginning in the 1880s, he moved toward anarchism, participating in the founding convention of the (largely anarcho-syndicalist) International Working People's Association in Pittsburgh in 1883. An advocate of the collectivization of the means of production, Spies defined socialism or anarchism—the two terms were synonymous in his eyes—as a form of universal cooperation that entailed the abolition of capitalism. Accused of having been the author of the anarchist flier calling for the protest at Haymarket Square (the text included the call "Workingmen, to Arms!"), he maintained his anarchist convictions before the court. Shortly before his execution, he wrote to the reactionary governor of Illinois, Richard Oglesby, begging him to take just one life, his own.

Albert Parsons, born in the United States, had fought for the Union in the Civil War. Like Spies, he had started out as a member of the Socialist Labor Party but later moved on to anarcho-syndicalism. His analyses of capitalism and of class struggle were close to Marxism, but he was a firm believer in anarchism—which he defined as the struggle against the domination of one human over another—and he situated anarchism as the opposite of what he designated "statist socialism." Like his libertaire comrades, Parsons believed in workers' self-defense and supported efforts to form a workers' militia.

Adolph Fischer was another German immigrant; he and his friend George Engel edited the newspaper *Der Anarchist*, whose motto was "We Hate Authority." In his writings, he defended anarchist communism against attacks by some of Proudhon's supporters, whom he described as "middle-class Anarchists." According to him, the movement's objective was the abolition of the state, and on the economic front, "a communist or cooperative method of production." George Engel, also born in Germany, had followed the same path, in just a few years, from "electoral socialism" to the anarchism of the International Working People's Association. When the bomb exploded in Haymarket Square, he had been at home playing cards. He was nevertheless sentenced to death. Shortly before his execution, he sent a letter to Governor Oglesby in which he refused to beg for a commutation of his sentence: "I protest against a commutation of my sentence and demand either liberty or death. I renounce any kind of mercy."[2]

Louis Lingg was the youngest of the condemned men. He had arrived from Germany only a year before the events at Haymarket Square. A member of a carpenters' union, he had helped organize the union militia. His speech before the court has become a classic of American anarchist literature.[3] To escape the gallows, he killed himself with a cigar filled with dynamite, which a friend had smuggled in to him.

It is of interest to note that among those who mobilized in defense of the Chicago anarchists was Eleanor Marx, who had been traveling in the United States for a few short months in 1886. In a November 1886 speech, she denounced the trial as being "one of the most infamous legal murders that has ever been perpetrated." If the accused were executed, she proclaimed, "we may say of the executioners, what my father said of those who massacred the people of Paris: 'Its exterminators history has already nailed to that pillory from which all the prayers of their priests will not avail to redeem them.'"[4]

The Second International, at its 1889 congress in Paris, chose the first of May as the date for an international holiday commemorating the struggle for the eight-hour day. Over the years, as the more conservative union elements and the reformists downgraded May Day to a "Festival of Labor," the anarchist and Marxist Left kept the memory of the Haymarket Martyrs alive, making the day a celebration of international struggle and solidarity. The legacy of Haymarket played an important role in the founding of the Industrial Workers of the World a generation later. A revolutionary trade-unionist movement in the United States, its members, commonly known as "Wobblies," advocated for direct action and the general strike. The largest strike organized by the Wobblies was the successful textile workers' strike in Lawrence, Massachusetts, in 1912. The two primary organizers were two Italian-American activists, the anarcho-syndicalist Joseph Ettor, and the Marxist socialist Arturo Giovannitti. They were both imprisoned, but, thanks to a large public pressure campaign, released by the courts.

The early American Communists, such as John Reed, William Z. Foster, James Cannon, and Bill Haywood (all of whom, save Reed, were Wobblies) often paid tribute to Albert Parsons and his comrades. Throughout the twentieth century, all revolutionary branches of the labor movement were familiar with the Haymarket Martyrs; they were a shared point of reference. But it was the anarchists, most of all, that succeeded in making the dead of 1886–87 a rallying cry for the revolutionary world.

Revolutionary Trade Unionism and the Charter of Amiens (1906)

Amiens, 1906. In France, the story of the birth of the revolutionary trade-unionist movement is one that has stood the test of time. The Confédération générale du travail (CGT; General Confederation of Labor), made its first appearance at the dawn of the twentieth century and quickly set the world of French labor ablaze. In its own way, the CGT's rise reengaged with the unifying movement brought about by the creation of the First International some forty years earlier, even as it breathed life into a new radicalism. This sudden eruption of union activity also marked an end to the quest for self-representation for the exploited and the oppressed. For this reason, the period is well known among both Marxists and libertaires.

The genesis of the CGT did not come out of any particular Marxist or anarchist movement. Moreover, its creation did not make for unanimous support in either of the two political families. But its birth owed much to the work of a generation of anarchist activists, and revolutionary Marxism, in turn, owed much to a generation of revolutionary trade unionists who ended up adherents of its theories. Indeed, at the beginning the CGT was rather libertaire in tone, most notably in that its operation gave a central place to the base of the organization, rather than its top. The anarchists who actively participated in the union's creation, and had therefore broken with the strategy of individual acts of political violence, had a hand in this.

(Let us recall that the early 1890s were very turbulent years, shaken by "anarchist" attacks, with the anarchists in turn clamped down on by the "villainous laws."[1]) Fernand Pelloutier (1867–1901), for example, played a critical role in the movement for the establishment of trade union halls, and even became secretary of its federation in 1895. He saw trade unionism as an alternative to individualist anarchism, which amounted to committing thefts and burglaries, in accordance with the theory of "individual reclamation" or even acts of terrorism and assassinations in the name of "propaganda by the deed."[2] Émile Pouget (1860–1931), too, strove to inject anarchism with a new momentum via syndicalism, becoming deputy secretary of the CGT and editor of its official weekly paper *La Voix du peuple* from 1900 on, even while publishing the formidable anarchist pamphlet *Le Père peinard*.

The emulation produced by revolutionary trade unionism also gave rise, in the wake of its atypical development, to unparalleled Marxist activists. Certain anarchists in the CGT gradually broke away from the ideals that they had started with in favor of a more genuine Marxism, far off the beaten path of the existent political parties. Among them were Pierre Monatte (1881–1960) and Alfred Rosmer (1877–1964), who were particularly active in the leadership of the CGT and in the launching of the journal *Vie ouvrière*, which they created in 1909.

The root cause of this gradual shift was World War I. Faced with a conflict that transformed people into cannon fodder, and with the Sacred Union quickly corrupting the workers' movement, radical syndicalists and internationalist Marxists came to know each other better.[3] They found themselves united at conferences like Zimmerwald (September 1915) and Kienthal (April 1916) to hold up the flag of antiwar internationalist socialism against all odds.

In 1917, the Russian Revolution opened up new prospects and brought the two points of view even closer together. The Bolsheviks even tried, at one time, to formalize these connections through the creation of the Red International of Labor Unions, commonly known as the Profintern, in 1921. The organization attempted to bring together radical trade unionists and the left wings of large union organizations, even while acting as an activist incubator for the creation of the communist parties then forming across Europe.

In the trade-unionist melting pot that shook the world in the early twentieth century, the rise of the CGT occupies a particular place and remains a remarkable story. It was the result of the confluence of two grassroots movements: the Fédération nationale des syndicats (National Federation of Unions)—which came out of a growth in the number of solidarity and mutual aid funds developed within businesses—and from 1892 onward, the Fédération des bourses du travail (Federation of Trade Union Halls). These trade union halls were places officially designated for the workers, assigned to them and allocated to their exclusive use. They spread throughout the country and were created in numerous cities. The push to unite the two federations led to the initial foundation of the CGT in Limoges in 1895; this feat was finalized seven years later in 1902 in Montpellier.

The French originality of syndicalism stems from this twofold nature—both professional, as an organization for unionizing businesses, and geographic, as an organization promoting the creation of trade union halls. The rapid establishment of these halls throughout France during the 1890s brought on a veritable craze among the French working class, diverting syndicalism from a potentially corporative trajectory, one in which its only interest was the defense of its affiliated trades and those who made their livings by them. For this reason, the contribution of the trade union halls was a decisive factor—huge numbers of workers played an active, local part in building the trade-unionist movement, controlling and directing it in an unprecedented way, at the grassroots level, by their direct involvement.

The trade union hall movement had its roots in Paris, as if the vindictive spirits of the Communards continued to hang over the city even after the ferocious repression of 1871. It was in 1875 that the workers presented the Paris city council with a collective petition for the creation of a public space specifically designed to receive the groups of laborers who went out looking for work each morning—a place to meet and share information, such as the number and type of jobs available, their wages, and so on. After the 1884 passage of the Waldeck-Rousseau law, unions were legalized and regulated. The issue was debated over the next several years: the intention to create the Paris trade union hall, subsidized by the city, was recorded in 1887, and the first hall founded shortly thereafter. The building itself would not be opened until 1892, on Rue du Château d'eau in Paris. The same year, the Fédération des Bourses du travail was created under Pelloutier's direction. After 1887 and the Parisian example, the movement had spread like wildfire to all the other cities in France: Nîmes, Marseille, then Lyon, Toulouse, Saint-Étienne, Toulon, Montpellier, Sète, Béziers, Nice, Cholet.... Union halls were set up by the dozens, filling a social vacuum and responding to a concrete demand from the working class. They provided a place to rest before the day's work, to hold meetings and debates, and to organize for the defense of the workers' interests. The management of these halls was carried out by the workers themselves. The city governments made spaces available to them and allocated them their own funds, most notably for the publication of newspapers. For the local authorities, this arrangement presented an advantage: they had all the leaders of the labor movement gathered together in one place and knew of their plans, rather than having to seek out and discover underground revolutionary movements. This was the only benefit for the state. All attempts at interference in the function of the trade union halls were systematically rejected in favor of workers' self-management.

The birth of the CGT in 1895 marked the advent of an exceptional era of trade unionism, and a crowning achievement in the epic of self-management: twenty years of revolutionary trade unionism, proclaimed without apology, demonstrating a beautiful workers' autonomy.

The Charter of Amiens, adopted on October 13, 1906, at the ninth congress of the CGT, reaffirmed this singularity. A veritable profession of radical syndicalist faith, the charter was not only a declaration of the unions' independence from the political parties, but first and foremost a response to the reformist evolution of the socialism of the day. So much so that, from the beginning, the text of the charter shows it to be highly political. In large part, it serves as the CGT's answer to the founding of the Section française de l'Internationale ouvrière (French Section of the Workers' International) in 1905. This new political party intended to unify the two existent socialist parties, one reformist and one revolutionary, one Jauresian, and one Guesdiste.[4] For many radical labor activists, the French Section of the Workers' International seemed to be drifting away from the spirit of the First International and the Commune, as elected socialists began taking seats in Parliament, and Alexandre Millerand became the first socialist to accept a cabinet position in the government of the Third Republic (1899–1902). In short, it seemed that socialism was entering the mainstream.

Amiens was the CGT's opportunity to make clear where they stood. In ten years, they had managed to build a union outside the control of political organizations, at great cost and with great struggle. Let us remember that the CGT in France was not created for the sole purpose of bringing the workers together in defense of their professional interests. One of its founding principles, essential to its creation, was to offer the workers a different social and political solution than the one offered by the socialism of the political parties—a solution that the revolutionary trade unionists demanded return to the hands of the working class, and not to socialist politicians. Essentially, the CGT was built as an act of defiance toward the parties, which first took the form of rejecting all political manipulation.

The first "birth" of the CGT, in Limoges in 1895, had already set the confederation on the path to independence from the socialists' grasp. Behind the rejection of institutionalization was the strong conviction that the union was the natural, legitimate, and "pure" organ of the proletariat *as a class*, as opposed to the interclass nature of political parties, which necessarily bring together people of all social strata. The CGT was also strongly influenced by the trade union hall movement, directed by the anarchist Fernand Pelloutier, which was openly hostile to reformist parties. In Pelloutier's view, syndicalism was the best bulwark of socialist ideas against their institutionalization in political parties. In his "Letter to Anarchists," written in 1899, he sums up his thoughts: "Currently, our position in the socialist world is this: banned from 'the Party' because we, no less revolutionary than Vaillant or Guesde, equally resolute supporters of the abolition of individual property, are nevertheless what they [the politicians] are not: full-time rebels, truly godless men, without master and without homeland."

The Charter of Amiens symbolized the proclamation of a revolutionary trade unionism that would resist the onslaught of the socialists. It was also a response to their advances. Initially, it was the director of the Textile Federation, a follower of Guesde named Renard, who proposed a motion for the rapprochement of the CGT with social democracy. Thus, he invited the standardization of union activity: the CGT would handle economic questions, and the parties would handle political ones. This motion garnered only 34 votes, with 736 against. The resolution now known to history as the Charter of Amiens, was in fact the reply to delegate Renard by two of the principal leaders of the CGT, Victor Griffuelhes (1874–1922) and Émile

Pouget—two men with two different political backgrounds and one vision for the union. Griffuelhes, a Blanquist, had been secretary of the CGT since 1901; Pouget, a libertaire, was the former editor of *Le Père peinard*.[5] Their motion (*"Outside of all political schools*, the CGT groups together all workers conscious of the fight to be carried out for the disappearance of the salaried and of employers") was approved by a wide margin—834 for, and only 8 against.[6] This vote probably does not reflect the exact balance of power within the CGT at the time. As a matter of fact, the system of delegation representing each union on an equal footing, regardless of the size of the business—and therefore the number of employees—favored small businesses and workshops, which were traditionally more radicalized than the newer, bigger units of industrial production. In these, which had just been born with the rise of capitalism, the workers had only recently (and still timidly) gotten involved in the class struggle. The revolutionary current thus had the advantage. Additionally, it is clear that this motion was approved not only by revolutionary trade unionists. It also won the votes of many reformist trade unionists who had voted to protest a potential subordination of the CGT to the French Section of the Workers' International. Beyond the balance of power between reformist and revolutionary, this vote reflects an incontestable reality and an undeniable political aspiration: in affirming its independence from parliamentary socialism, the CGT was not shying away from political questions. On the contrary, it was demanding them. This vote was an affirmation of the specificity of the French syndicalism on the international scene, distinguished by its radical and revolutionary character. Except for the Industrial Workers of the World in the United States, the Confederación Nacional del Trabajo (National Confederation of Labor) in Spain, and the Unione Sindacale Italiana (Italian Syndicalist Union or Italian Workers' Union) in Italy to lesser extent, few mass trade-unionist organizations have adopted this approach.[7] It is an approach marked by a twofold task, which the union then took up: to defend, from that day forward, the interests of the workers against the bosses; to claim for tomorrow the vision of a society definitively rid of capitalist exploitation.

The Spanish Revolution (1936–37): The Red and Black Revolution

Barcelona, 1936. The radical memory can sometimes be selective and simplify the complexity of events. It is generally understood, for example, that the 1917 Revolution was the accomplishment of the Bolsheviks, and the Spanish Revolution of 1936 that of the libertaires. This, however, is a simplistic reduction of both cases to the tendency that was in a position to influence the course of events—to the detriment of the other, which by definition could not also have been the primary actor. Yet, beyond the conflicts and ruptures between Bolsheviks and anarchists, the connections between these two families have indeed endured through each of these revolutions.

Spain in 1936 was not only the theater of a heroic war against Francoism and the fascisms of Europe, not only the tragic missed meeting of the resistance to the fascist threat, of the struggle of the International Brigades, which might have saved the entire world from the great disaster of the Second World War. More than a simple rehearsal for 1939–45, the war in Spain was a revolution—a genuine revolution from below, distinguished by the propulsion of the people to the front of the stage of history. Its achievements were eminently social: the collectivization of the land by the peasants, the socialized reappropriation of the factories by workers' councils, the requisition of public transit by the workers and the general population.

Figure 2. Poster by Arturo Ballester for the National Committee of the CNT, 1936. Reproduced with permission from *Espagne 36: Les officines des combattant-e-s de la liberté* (Chaucre, FR: Éditions libertaires, 2005).

On July 19, 1936, an armed populist revolt was set in motion by the Confederación Nacional del Trabajo (CNT; National Confederation of Labor), a libertaire union created in 1910 and more than 1.5 million strong. This uprising was provoked by the military coup d'état of General Franco, who denied the recent electoral victory of the leftist Popular Front on February 16. This abrupt acceleration of the class struggle was the end result of a long historical process in Spain: a historic general strike in 1917, thwarted and followed by years of political authoritarianism and repression by the bosses; the dictatorship of Primo Rivera from 1923 to 1930, marked by clandestine activity, fantastic exploits, minor armed actions, and the rebirth of collective struggles; the stillborn Republic of 1931, antisocial and disappointing; the return of a vengeful Right in 1933; the failed revolution of October 1934....

These were just a few of the political jolts suffered by a Spanish society undergoing radical transformation, violent to the point of bringing on its own paralysis, its profound division and even its implosion. The opposing parties were conservatives against progressives, the nobility and the owning classes against the working classes, with both sides more or less expecting a climax that had, because of the circumstances, become inevitable. As a result, the failed revolution of 1934, far from demoralizing the workers, was not perceived as a total defeat but rather as an aborted attempt, logically calling for another.

Beginning in the spring of 1935, the workers' movement, despite heavy persecution—more than thirty thousand of its activists were in prison—went on the offensive again. Shortly after the electoral victory of the Popular Front—an alliance of socialists, communists, and republicans—fascist elements of the military under the direction of General Francisco Franco attempted to seize power on July 18, 1936. On July 19, a revolutionary populist uprising in the major cities of Spain (Barcelona, Madrid, etc.) prevented the Francoist counterrevolution from claiming victory—this was the start of the civil war. All eyes turned to Spain, and the world, troubled by the ascent of Nazism in Germany, of fascism in Italy, and of the Stalinist purges in the USSR, held its breath.

Of the year 1939, the official histories record the fall of the Spanish Republic and Franco's victory: Barcelona fell in January, and then Madrid in March. It was also the start of World War II. But the end of the 1930s, before the tipping point, could just as well be dated earlier, according to another chronology: that of a revolutionary cycle that came to an end in the month of May 1937. It had begun on July 19, 1936, with the populist uprising across Spain. It was brutally ended by the coordinated actions of the Spanish republican bourgeoisie and the Partit Socialista Unificat de Catalunya (PSUC; United Socialist Party of Catalonia), which grouped together Catalan Communists and Socialists, under the Stalinists' hegemony, nearly two years before the final collapse of the Spanish Republic.

A sock puppet of Stalin and the NKVD, his secret police, the Spanish Communist Party became particularly ruthless during this period, torturing and eliminating many of its opponents, even within the ranks of its own combatants against Francoism. The Kremlin wanted a stabilized Spain, not one convulsed by uncontrolled bursts of revolutionary activity that could upset its games of international diplomacy. Stalin did not want to overly upset Nazi Germany at the time, a strategy that the Nazi-Soviet Nonaggression Pact, signed in August 1939, would bring to light.

The uprising of July 19, 1936, and the proclamation of the Spanish Republic was lost on those communists under the thumb of the Comintern. The movement resisting the Francoist putsch was led by the members of the CNT, the anarchist organization, and the members of the Partido Obrero de Unificación Marxista (POUM; Workers' Party of Marxist Unification), founded in 1935 from the fusion of the Bloque

Obrero y Campesino, a dissident communist organization led by Joaquín Maurín, and the Izquierda Comunista de España, a Trotskyist movement led by Andreu Nin. In Moscow's eyes, the Iberian troublemakers represented a danger that needed to be eliminated. Thus, Andreu Nin, one of the leading figures of the anti-Stalinist Marxist camp, was removed from his post as a minister of the Catalan regional government, then arrested, and finally murdered by a Stalinist commando unit in June 1937. In less than a year, the bureaucratic counterrevolution imposed itself on—and overtook—the revolution. Over the summer of 1936, the CNT allowed the republican government of the socialist Francisco Largo Caballero to set itself up, in the expectation that it would do nothing more than endorse the decisions made by the grassroots. But this failed to take into account the intentions of the Communist Party and the republican bourgeoisie, hostile to Franco but equally recalcitrant about the revolutionary process then underway. This unnatural pairing, bourgeois and communist, put its hopes in the government to normalize the situation as quickly as possible. Thus, the counterrevolution progressively began to interfere in political life, gumming up the works of the revolution. In September 1936, the Committee of Antifascist Militias, the organ of the revolutionary armed struggle, was dissolved. The Ken Loach film *Land and Freedom* immortalizes the drama that was the disarmament of the militias in particularly heartrending scenes: the power was taken away from the people in arms and given in its entirety to the republican government, which removed a thorn from the side of the bourgeoisie, and a considerable one at that. The benevolence of the CNT leadership toward the republican government is astonishing.

In November 1936, the anarchist José Buenaventura Durruti was killed by a stray bullet; his death was likely accidental, but the exact circumstances have never been explained. In addition to his military successes, he had known how to show his autonomy in regard to the government, and had strongly opposed the militarization of the libertaire militias. His death left behind a great number of "orphaned" revolutionaries. In December, the POUM was driven out of the Catalan government. In early May 1937, a workers' uprising broke out in Barcelona, led by the CNT and the POUM to counter the attempt by the state police to seize the central telephone exchange, a building which had until then been under the workers' control. The revolt was finally put down, defanged in part by the appeals for calm launched by the "CNT-ist" ministers of the government. In mid-May, the resignation of the Caballero government, deemed too far left by the Stalinists and unable to lead the crackdown on the POUM, led to the nomination of Juan Negrín as its new head, who had all the support of the communists. That was the final turn of events. With the assassination of Andreu Nin in June, the revolution's fate was sealed.

The Spanish Revolution, then, is not the dream synthesis of Marxism and anarchism—far from it. We must not look to embellish history. The POUM and the CNT, in any case, were not defending the same political stance on unity or electoral participation, among other issues. Yet the fates of many militants from these two branches became intertwined in the heart of the revolutionary process.

Thus, the French surrealist poet Benjamin Péret (1889–1959), who was one of the representatives of the Fourth International in Spain, chose in May 1937 to fight in the ranks of the Durruti column.[1] Likewise, some of the anarchists openly affirmed their solidarity with the POUM, who were squaring off against the Stalinist crackdown and paying the price in blood. Such was the case with Camilo Berneri (1897–1937), an Italian anarchist taking part in the Spanish Revolution who was assassinated by the NKVD in 1937, who declared: "It must be said loud and clear that he who insults and slanders the POUM and demands its repression is a saboteur of the antifascist struggle and will not be tolerated."[2]

From a certain point of view, the Stalinist counterrevolution brought the two currents closer together. The revolutionary Marxist writer George Orwell, himself enlisted in the ranks of the POUM militia, highlighted this proximity, this reciprocal "instinct" for solidarity.[3] He confessed that "as far as my purely personal preferences went I would have liked to join the Anarchists," summarizing the situation this way: "During the first two months of the war it was the Anarchists more than anyone else who had saved the situation, and much later than this the Anarchist militia, in spite of their indiscipline, were notoriously the best fighters among the purely Spanish forces. From about February 1937 onwards the Anarchists and the P.O.U.M. could to some extent be lumped together."[4] And indeed, at the barricades thrown up during the May Days revolt against the government's attempt to take the telephone exchange in Barcelona, the passwords to be allowed through were "CNT-FAI" or "CNT-POUM."

In truth, Durruti's unexplained death in November of 1936 had dampened the hope for an authentic libertaire revolution. Andreu Nin's disappearance in June 1937 (and assassination by the NKVD), marked a major turning point for the revolution. The POUM understood the situation and proposed a common revolutionary front: "CNT-POUM." This front had already existed since January, initiated by the Juventud Comunista Ibérica, the POUM's youth organization. On May 3, the POUM suggested to the CNT that they take inspiration from this model and unite the CNT, the Federación Anarquista Ibérica (FAI; Iberian Anarchist Federation), the POUM, and the socialist Left—all the political movements represented in the Barcelona uprising—into a common nexus of power.[5] Convinced that the show of force of the Barcelona revolt had been enough, to borrow their words, "to show their teeth" to the central government, the leadership of the CNT, in a considerably hegemonic position over the working class, categorically refused. In rejecting this offer, they interred, without

knowing it, the hope of a new impetus for the revolutionary process. Numerous debates shook the CNT during these
weeks: the Friends of Durruti, an anarchist collective created
in March 1937, severely criticized the CNT's decision. Though
the merger of the CNT with the POUM was not made, its failure
was more for reasons of circumstance than political ones: the
groups were not present in the same regions, but rather were
separated by the front lines of the war. However, the POUM
went quite a distance with the libertaire youth movement,
which had also criticized the CNT's refusal.

After the years have passed, with their share of regrets
and frustrations, it is tempting to remember the hypothetical
Durruti-Nin duo as representing the two faces of the Spanish
Revolution. Durruti was not a Marxist; he was a committed
anarchist. All the same, he opted for some of Marxism's organizing principles, a thorny subject among the libertaires as it
implicitly raised the question of taking power. As for Andreu
Nin, he and his close companion and comrade Joaquín Maurín
had come directly out of the revolutionary trade-unionist movement of the CNT. Active in the CNT from 1918, Nin had played
an essential role at the 1919 congress where the question of
supporting the Russian Revolution and joining the Comintern
had been discussed. Nin represented the "Soviet" period of the
CNT; he had joined its general secretariat in March 1921. From
April 1921 to June 1922 the CNT was a member of the Profintern,
which brought together revolutionary unions from around
the world. Then, under pressure from the anarchists, the CNT
reasserted its independence.

Initially appointed by the CNT, and then as a completely
independent agent, Nin had busied himself about Moscow
between 1921 and 1930 at the offices of the Profintern. There he
mingled with many revolutionary trade unionists and libertaires who had been won over to communism by the October
Revolution—they were flocking there from around the world,
including France. It was there that he met Pierre Monatte and

Alfred Rosmer. Rosmer must have found in the pair formed by Nin and Maurín during the Spanish Civil War an Iberian reflection of his and Monatte's duo: "The [representatives] of a new generation of syndicalists, less inclined to endless discussions and better prepared to understand the profound meaning of the October Revolution."[6] Out of the debates that had taken place in the Comintern came clusters of political proximity. Such was the case with Nin and Trotsky, who had a strong but complicated relationship. Their political collaboration, well-documented by numerous international sources, ended with the establishment of the POUM in 1935, which Trotsky condemned. He was not convinced of the need to form a separate movement, working in conjunction with Maurín's party, which he deemed centrist—neither revolutionary nor reformist. Despite this, in his work devoted to the POUM, Wilebaldo Solano insists that Trotsky attentively and sympathetically followed the epic of the anti-Stalinist Marxist current, particularly as it was targeted for repression by Moscow.

When all is said and done, this revolution must be recorded in the too-numerous chapters of history that tell of revolutions uncompleted or betrayed. It also forms a shared history. The instincts of property are tenacious, even within the various lines of descent of revolutionary politics. Our memories, too, must be collectivized. Without denying the crucial and central role of the Bolshevik Party in Russia in 1917, or that of the CNT in Spain in 1936, it must be noted that these two revolutions are neither the preserve of the one, nor the private lands of the other, but rather two shared experiences from which we must learn. All those who still wish, today, to change the world must take inspiration from them.

May 68

Nanterre, 1968. Most historians agree that the formation of the Movement of 22 March (M-22) was the starting point for the student unrest that led to the events of May 68, as it came to be known. Yet, as we know, this movement was formed thanks to the convergence of opinion and action of anarchists and Marxists, their two most prominent spokespeople being the libertaire Daniel Cohn-Bendit and the "Trotsko-Guevarist" Daniel Bensaïd, who was also one of the founders of the Jeunesse communiste révolutionnaire (Revolutionary Communist Youth), or JCR.

At the root of the formation of the Movement of 22 March was the arrest of a student from Nanterre, an activist with the "Jecrew," as the JCR was called, Xavier Langlade, who had led a direct action against the headquarters of American Express; some windows had been broken and the slogan "FNL vaincra" (the Viet Cong will win) had been painted. Hundreds of students gathered at the University of Nanterre on March 22 and decided to occupy the university's administration building and demand Langlade's release. Over the following days, the rally grew and a group of activists decided to create the Movement of 22 March—the name was probably inspired (not without a touch of irony) by the 26th of July Movement in Cuba.

In the book he hurriedly wrote with Henri Weber in the immediate aftermath of "les événements,"[1] Daniel Bensaïd described the M-22 as a movement created by the unaffiliated, the anarchists, and activists from the JCR "at the cost of reciprocal concessions and on the basis of a common political experience which was the starting point for the discussions, without agreement on a 'line' being a precondition for action."[2] Much later, in his 2004 memoirs he defined the M-22 as a movement that was "anti-imperialist (solidarity with the Indochinese and Cuban peoples), anti-bureaucratic (solidarity with the Polish students and the Prague Spring), and anti-capitalist (solidarity with the [striking] workers of Caen and Redon)"[3]—a list to which antiauthoritarian must necessarily be added.

In their book devoted to the players of May 68, which collected a number of eyewitness accounts of the events, Hervé Hamon and Patrick Rotman speak of the M-22 as "a movement, a melting pot, without manifesto, without official hierarchy, without elected leaders."[4] Cohn-Bendit happened to come into a leadership role because he was "libertaire enough for the anarchists, and thoughtful enough for the Leninists."[5] The political heterogeneity of the movement was obvious: "If they sat down at a table to talk doctrine, conditions, or theory, they wouldn't last ten minutes together. The only cement that held them together was action."[6] The depiction is a bit exaggerated, for without a minimum of political agreement, the movement would not have been able to engage in actions, nor hold meetings or publish handouts together. Hamon and Rotman are interested in the role played by Bensaïd, who represented the JCR within the M-22: "He liked and respected the spontaneity of it. Right away, he grasped the originality of the approach, understood that it shattered the age-old activist ritual in just the right way, that it jumped across the divisions between factions. He preached unity, stuck to Cohn-Bendit, whose point of view he more or less shared: the members of the M-22 are all those who accept the initiatives decreed together."[7]

It was therefore not by accident that Daniel Bensaïd became the link between revolutionary Marxists and libertaires. Born and raised in Toulouse, a city heavily influenced by the political culture of the anarchist exiles from the Spanish Civil War, he integrated this history at a young age into his vision of the fight for a socialist society. As he recounts in his memoirs, his mother's bistro was frequented by Spanish refugees: "I listened all ears to the epic tales of the Spanish civil war."[8]

If the libertaire current around Cohn-Bendit accepted, without too much difficulty, the idea of cooperating with revolutionary Marxists, it was also because theirs was a movement interested by the ideas of heterodox Marxists like Henri Lefebvre, Herbert Marcuse, and of course, Guy Debord. They had certainly not forgotten Kronstadt,[9] but Marxism per se was not an obstacle—to the contrary.

The M-22 played an important role in the student movement in May, and anarchist ideas had a wide influence in May and beyond. Although the anarchist groups that were organized—for example, the Fédération anarchiste—had only a limited role, many themes from anarchist culture held considerable attraction, such as antiauthoritarianism, the rejection of political organizations or bureaucratic unions, the valorization of spontaneity, and the opposition to the state and its institutions.

Many observers were shocked by the presence, in the demonstrations and on the barricades, of the black flag alongside the red. The English journalist Daniel Singer, a Luxemburgist Marxist and the author of one of the most interesting books on May 68, noted: "In the French May Movement there were discernible antiauthoritarian echoes of Proudhon as well as of Bakunin."[10] For him, "the revival of vague forms of anarchism" was "a healthy reaction against the bureaucratic degeneration of the official labor movement," a movement which seemed to have forgotten its revolutionary and antiauthoritarian origins.[11]

It was not by accident then, that anarchists and revolutionary Marxists met, within a crowd of unorganized youth driven by revolt and indignation, upon the barricades in the Latin Quarter of Paris during the *nuit de feu* (night of fire) on May 9. In opposition were the "orthodox Trotskyists" of the Parti communiste internationaliste, and the Maoist Union des jeunesses communistes marxistes-léninistes, who turned their backs on these "petty bourgeois" actions. Not to mention, of course, the Stalinist Parti communiste français, which ceaselessly denounced the "tiny groups" who were "playing power games." Nothing could have been further from the attitude of young people who discovered "under the paving stones, the beach."[15] Beyond their (very real) disagreements, the revolutionary followers of the red flag and of the black found themselves quite naturally "on the same side of the barricades," both literally and figuratively.

This de facto alliance also appeared within the support for mass strikes—the most significant in modern French history—in May 1968, in the occupations of factories, in the criticism of union bureaucracy, and in the drive to form strike committees. To be sure, the libertaires and the JCR had only a limited influence on the labor movement, but certain segments of the working-class youth and some critical currents within the unions were not insensitive to their calls for self-organization.

From Alterglobalization to Occupy Wall Street

Today, around the world. The first initiative that can be said to have paved the way for the alterglobalization movement was the Intercontinental (or indeed, "intergalactic," to use Subcomandante Marcos's ironic wording) Conference for Humanity and against Neoliberalism, convened by the Zapatista Army of National Liberation in the remote mountains of Chiapas, Mexico, in 1996.

History, however, records the direct ancestor of the movement as being the giant street demonstrations in Seattle, in late November and the first few days of December 1999, against the latest round of negotiations by the World Trade Organization (WTO), which had brought together representatives from more than a hundred countries. Tens of thousands of protestors clashed with the police over several days. The mobilization was very diverse, including everyone "from Teamsters to turtles"—meaning from truck drivers' unions to environmental activists dressed up in turtle costumes—as well as a mass of young people, including some anarchists and Marxists. One of the principal organizers of the WTO protests was the Direct Action Network, a horizontal libertaire network linking similar groups of activists for acts of nonviolent civil disobedience. Among the union activists, there were activists from *Labor Notes*, a movement driven by the revolutionary Marxists of the group Solidarity.

Two years after Seattle, in January 2001, the first World Social Forum (WSF) was held in the city of Porto Alegre, in the south of Brazil. The WSF was the joint initiative of a French team linked to the organization ATTAC (founded in the wake of the Seattle protests),[1] Bernard Cassen's newspaper *Le monde diplomatique*, and a Brazilian group linked to social movements that included Chico Whitaker and Oded Grajew. Behind the slogan "Another World Is Possible," the WSF wanted to present a visible alternative to the World Economic Forum, which was meeting that same week, as it does every year, in Davos, Switzerland. Those in attendance are the elite of the elite—bankers, politicians, entrepreneurs, and other capitalists "bleeding the world dry." Revolutionary Marxists, especially Brazilians, played a decisive role in the organization of the first WSF, most notably via the municipal government of Porto Alegre, a bastion of the Workers' Party at the time and the Democratic Socialist movement of which Raul Pont, the mayor himself, was a member. When the WSF left the city of Porto Alegre for its fourth iteration in 2004, other revolutionary Marxist activists took over, notably Éric Toussaint, head of the Committee for the Abolition of Illegitimate Debt (CADTM). One of the first books to take stock of the WSF's experience in Porto Alegre was published in 2003; it was the work of José Correa Leite, a Brazilian member of the Democratic Socialist movement, now called the Socialism and Liberty Party.[2]

Initially the libertaires were divided as to their participation in the WSF. Some libertaires—activists in various social movements, unions, peasants', and students' organizations—had chosen to be present at the first conference. In some cases, organized anarchist groups set up their own separate but parallel initiatives, particularly among the youth branches of the WSF, which enjoyed a certain autonomy. The annual and global event of the WSF was not devoid of the anarchist tendency.

These divisions were no longer on the agenda in any of the large alterglobalization protests that followed, be they gatherings against the conferences of the WTO or International Monetary Fund, or against the G8, as in Genoa in July 2001, or even the 2003 mobilizations against the war in Iraq, which continued throughout the decade. In the crowds of protestors—in Genoa there were hundreds of thousands of them—all the various strains of alterglobalization could be found, from leftist Catholics and Marxists to pacifists, anarchists, and environmentalists—the same diverse composition as the protests of the late 1990s. Among the organizations serving as links between these various tendencies, one of the most interesting was the English network Reclaim the Streets. A movement for nonviolent direct action, Reclaim the Streets refused all institutionalization. On June 19, 1999, the day before the opening of the G7, they paralyzed the City, London's central business district, with a protest of ten thousand people.

In the early 2000s, however, the anarchists split into two distinct tendencies: a smaller current that supported violent actions, better known as the black bloc, a largely uncoordinated nebula of individuals united in action; and a larger current, encompassing a wide spectrum from devoted pacifists to supporters of the insurrectionary general strike. Revolutionary Marxists, who are not pacifists in the least, tend in general to prefer unified mass actions and to be wary of the black bloc's actions, which tend to be organized in small groups. These actions can, in extreme circumstances, have tragic unintended consequences. In Greece in 2010, for example, during a massive protest, some participants—very probably affiliated with the black bloc, who are usually the ones to engage in this sort of action—threw Molotov cocktails into a bank. In the ensuing blaze, three employees were killed. The arsonists accepted responsibility, but so did the bank manager, who had chosen to lock the doors rather than allow his employees to join the protest.[3]

In Egypt, a year and a half after the beginning of the Arab Spring that ousted Hosni Mubarak, attempts to organize in black bloc were led by numerous groups of young people, including several groups of soccer fans. They aimed to resist the repressive assaults on the occupation of Tahrir Square, in the center of Cairo, by the police and the militias in the pay of the new regime. In 2012, for those groups threatened by the changing circumstances of the revolutionary process, it was a matter of protecting themselves from counterrevolutionary violence, whether it came from the army or from the government of Mohamed Morsi, with its strong ties to the Muslim Brotherhood. In late 2012 and 2013, the repression came down with a heavy hand not only on those opposed to the Brotherhood, but also on Egyptian anarchists and Marxists, like the Libertarian Socialist Movement or the Revolutionary Socialists.

One last recent example is the Movimento Passe Livre (Movement for Free Public Transit) in Brazil. The fight against a hike in transit fares unleashed a vast and impressive popular mobilization in Brazil in June 2013. The movement was founded in January 2005, at the WSF in Porto Alegre. It is a federative, "horizontal" network of autonomous collectives. The organization has libertaire anticapitalist leanings, but the activists who constitute its membership come from different political perspectives: Trotskyists, anarchists, and supporters of the alterglobalization and Zapatista movements; some, with a touch of humor, self-identify as "anarcho-Marxist punks."

The anarchists have contributed much to the alterglobalization movement: a radical opposition to capitalism and statism, a healthy distrust of the bureaucracies of institutionalized unions, a horizontal praxis opposed to the verticalism of the political parties of the Left, a spirit of initiative, far off the beaten path of the traditional labor movement. Their principal disagreements with the revolutionary Marxists, paradoxically, concern questions of "democratic process"—should decisions be made by consensus or by majority rule? Should we create permanent popular assemblies or elect delegates? Another source of contention, this one of a strategic nature: will the future be built upon the local experiments of liberated communities, or political struggle against the system from within? Which is correct—small-scale or large-scale? The Marxist and anarchist camps remain divided on this crucial point, which we will revisit shortly.[4]

The same qualities and contradictions, more or less, can be found in the (heavily anarchist-influenced) movements keeping the alterglobalization struggle alive today—the protests of the Indignés in Europe and the initiative of Occupy Wall Street, first in New York, and then in numerous cities throughout the United States. These movements take up certain themes (for example, the critique of neoliberalism and financial capitalism) from the WSF, but also invent new forms of action, often inspired by the Arab Spring, such as the occupations of central urban spaces. What began with Tahrir Square in Cairo was later taken up in Plaza del Sol in Madrid, Syntagma Square in Athens, Zuccotti Park in New York, and Taksim Square in Istanbul.

The two young Catalan academics and activists with the group Izquierda Anticapitalista, Josep Maria Antentas and Esther Vivas, stress this dynamic in their book *Planeta Indignado: Ocupando el futuro*.[5] One of the "multiple meanings" of the occupation of public spaces is its taking on a uniquely democratic character. It transforms "a place historically constructed for the public display of power, via its emblematic buildings or monuments, into a place of protest," and subverts the normal distribution of public space—transforming it, at the same time, into a *democratic* space.[6] The deliberations that take place there have within them a profound search for political self-representation, a theme as dear to anarchists as it is for those Marxists who believe in self-management. Thus, though these two "rounds of the fight against global capitalism" take place in different contexts—the one, alterglobalization, in reaction to the triumphant neoliberalism of the early 1990s, and the other, the Indigné and Occupy movements, in opposition to the great capitalist crisis of 2008—these two cycles perpetuate each other and feed into each other within a single movement where social and democratic questions intermingle.[7] It is for this reason that activists from the red side and activists from the black side intermingle there too.

Portraits

Letter to Louise Michel
(1830–1905)

Dear Louise,

This letter probably would have annoyed you. You, the revolutionary who couldn't stand cults of personality. But you see, here in France, more than a hundred years after your death, those in power—who deserve our suspicion now more than ever—celebrate only the anniversaries of the conquerors. Napoleon still makes the headlines two centuries after his coronation. The Paris Commune, the first revolution led by and for the people, is no longer discussed—or very little, in any case. Yet the spring of 1871 gave the world a glimpse of what was then only an idea, proved that a society other than the one constructed by capitalism was possible. It was short-lived: only a few weeks. But when a revolution interrupts the flow of history, the units of time and measurement are thrown into turmoil—the experience must have seemed centuries to you and your comrades, and surely an eternity to the counter-revolutionaries of Versailles. An eternity condensed into a few lines in our history books, stunted by the compressor of a single, still-dominant way of thinking.

Today, if you only knew, the few streets that bear your name run alongside boulevards with the names of your vanquishers—Thiers, MacMahon.[1] Yes, Louise, the executioners of the Communards are still well established, and hardly

Figure 3: Louise Michel, lithograph by André Néraudan, 1880.
© Photothèque Hachette Livre.

anyone knows that they are responsible for the bloodbath
that cut down thirty thousand Parisians. Starving but proud,
exhausted by months of siege warfare, that multitude of anonymous Parisians is now and forever free. Today, in the 18th
arrondissement of Paris where you taught and defended the
Commune, I watch the tourists taking pictures of the Sacré-
Coeur. Most have no idea that this monument was built to
expunge subversive spirits like yours. In the twenty-first
century, the Versaillais (enemies of the Commune) live in
Neuilly-sur-Seine.[2] Rue Perronet, where for days on end you
fired on the enemy from atop a barricade to stop him from

taking the city's freedom, no longer bears the slightest trace of the bombardments that pummeled you and your comrades in your shelters, wounding your bodies and your dreams. Nearby, at Levallois where you are buried, the exploiters, with much help from the housing developers, have chased the riffraff from the city center. Despite it all, your shadow hangs over Levallois as it does all of the north of Paris, and carries with it the indefatigable hope of a more just, more emancipated world. The new Republic, propelled by the blossoming industrial bourgeoisie (and not by the fall of the Empire, ridiculed and defeated by the Prussians at Sédan on September 1, 1870), wanted nothing to do with this long-awaited change.[3]

This fact had already been made painfully clear to the Parisian proletariat in June 1848, when thousands of workers who thought their day had come were massacred in the streets. In 1871, the owning classes still hadn't changed their minds. Better, then, to collude with the *outside* enemy of old—the Prussians, who had always been social allies anyway, joined by the same financial appetites—than to enter into an unnatural union with the timeless enemy *within*—the people of Paris. "Rather Bismarck than Blanqui!" was the watchword of Thiers and his stooges.

Yet there they were, the people of Paris in this time of war, in possession of guns and cannons. It would not be easy for the Assemblée Nationale, which had withdrawn to Versailles, abandoning the city to the workers, to get them back. On March 17, 1871, they first sent their soldiers to take back your arms—though in truth, it was your destiny, more than your cannons, that they wanted to take away. Instead, they sparked the creation of the Commune—the momentum of the working class prevailed over the forces of reaction, insurrection over humiliation, solidarity between the soldiers they sent and those of the National Guard over repression. It was a revolution.[4] Of course, the Commune had plenty of trials and tribulations to overcome; it could not and did not succeed. But the Commune can boast of having forever opened a breach in the fortress of dominant ideas, of having forever proved that revolution and democracy can go hand in hand. Despite its limitations, the experiment of the Commune still resonates today, in the era of capitalist globalization, which makes the people pay for its crises, transforms everything into a commodity, even democracy itself. The egalitarian redistribution of wealth still necessitates its taking from the tiny minority of the powerful in order to restore it to the immense majority of the exploited, still demands that we defy the unchecked power these privileged few exert over the economy as they do over the whole of society. The democracy of the Commune functioned from the bottom up; it combined universal suffrage and direct democracy, guaranteeing a multiparty system, freedom of the press, and oversight and recallability of the elected.

Your name, Louise Michel, resounds like an affront in the ears of the adversaries of change and all those who would urge us to "be realistic." The conservatives of the Right, like those of the liberal Left, assert that all revolutions lead to blood-soaked tragedy—yet there is no one among them in France today that pretends not to know that the Communards' Wall in Père Lachaise Cemetery was once splattered with the blood of the revolutionary Communards, and not that of the reactionary Versaillais.[5] It matters little to them—our memories, too, are detestable in their eyes. Your determination made of you an eternally irredeemable element for the system. In the face of the court that was to send you to the penal colony, you looked the judges up and down and put the executioners of the Commune on trial instead, turned the world upside down on those notable and respectable members of society—all as a woman, in 1871! For you made this revolution a women's revolution, even a feminist one; the struggle for women's liberation was a major challenge within the communalist movement, as macho behavior was also widespread. Yet the first protests of September 1870 had been led by women. The female ambulance drivers of Montmartre, coming to help the wounded, picked up the rifles of the men on the ground to fight in their place and hold the barricade. Unbowed, militant, *pétroleuse*—you represented all that at once in the hateful and misogynistic imagination of the Versaillais world.[6] The leaders of that world could only have hated you.

You didn't see yourself as a martyr, nor as a secular saint, nor as a "red virgin." Certainly, you liked the smell of gunpowder, but you had nothing of the suicidal tendency that some experts like to ascribe to anyone—especially a woman—who dares to defy an army of the powerful. You were curious about life and you lived it fully and you believed in a better future; you, the poetess, the scientist's apprentice, the artist, the schoolteacher.

For you, the revolution was no passing affair, but a lifelong engagement. To be a revolutionary is to be one beyond all social and political fluctuations. Nearly a decade spent in the penal colony of New Caledonia couldn't kill your passion. And the Indigenous Kanak people who are still fighting for their independence remember you, the rare Communard to have supported them. And when you first returned from exile, still more ready for a fight, you braved the crackdowns stronger than before. When others were changing sides, you waved your black flag higher than before, in defiance of the courtroom and the prison. An anarchist, you didn't like sectarianism and preferred to align yourself foremost with the wide family of revolutionary movements. You liked to remind people: "For my part, I do not bother with particularist questions. I stand with all groups which attack the cursed edifice of the old society, whether with pickaxe, land mine, or fire."[7] Your struggle reaches us across the years and calls us to act, here and now.

It was my grandmother, a schoolteacher from Levallois, a town with mostly communist sympathies, who first told me about you, told me how you had defended the people. I don't think she was familiar with the whole of your struggle or your thought, but she thought of you as one of her own. You wanted to see "the heroes of legend of the times that are to come" rise up, and call on us to transform ourselves into "great chasers of stars."[8] Of course, the stars still seem very far away, but they shine brightly enough that some of us here still believe they're worth fighting for.

To you, Louise.

Yours in Revolution,

Olivier Besancenot

Pierre Monatte (1881–1960)

Some figures in the pantheon of the labor movement are more inconspicuous than others. Pierre Monatte is one such figure. Yet his story forms one of the most beautiful pages in the history of revolutionary syndicalism in France.

Heavily affected by the Dreyfus Affair,[1] Monatte was politicized in his youth by reading Zola and Hugo. He met militant anarchists and joined their ranks at a time when they were regularly making headlines with bombings and terrorist attacks. His preference, however, was for collective action and radical publications, like Émile Pouget's *Le Père peinard*, as well as *Le Libertaire, Les Temps nouveaux*, and *Pages libres*. He worked as a middle-school proctor, bookstore employee, and finally proofreader at a printshop—a post he held until his retirement—and became faithfully active in the revolutionary trade-unionist cause. He was swept up in the effervescence of the syndicalist movement, which had been thriving since the 1890s. Émile Pouget helped him onto the Federal Committee of Trade Union Halls in 1904. In 1907, at the International Anarchist Congress in Amsterdam, which brought together delegates from more than a dozen countries, the argument he engaged in with one of the great names of anarchism, the Italian Errico Malatesta, entered into the annals of radical labor history:

Revolutionary syndicalism, unlike socialism and anarchism which came before it, has found a place for itself more through action than through theory and it must be sought in action rather than in books. One would need to be blind not to see all that anarchism and syndicalism have in common. Both have the aim of the complete destruction of capitalism and the wage system by means of a social revolution.... The [First] International's motto [in 1864] was, you will recall, "the emancipation of the workers will be the task of the workers themselves," and it is still our motto, all of us.... The syndicate ... cannot and must not be anarchist, nor Guesdist, nor Allemanist, nor Blanquist, but simply of the workers.[2]

Monatte founded the journal *La Vie ouvrière* (Workers' life) in 1909. The name was a tribute to Fernand Pelloutier, who devoted his life to the founding of the Confédération générale du travail (CGT; General Confederation of Labor). Around the publication a strong friendship between Monatte and Alfred Rosmer was born, cemented by their resistance to the vicissitudes of the era. Rosmer, who was a "simple" clerk at the offices of the Paris municipal government, spoke several languages including English, and had contributed articles to *Les Temps nouveaux*. He had anarchist leanings, but as time went on he became more closely aligned with revolutionary trade unionism. On the eve of World War I, Monatte entrusted the publication of *La Vie ouvrière* to Rosmer, as he was conscripted and sent to the front, which took him away from his post for three years. The two of them worked in lockstep together. Their partnership symbolizes the saga of a generation of activists who were deeply revolutionary, and in more than name only. They were internationalists, too, internationalists always. Through thick and thin, they crossed chaotic, feverish years marked by frantic swings between hope and despair. Both held fast to

their engagements even as the era was plunged into a whirl-
wind of doubt and blindness, beginning with the blindness of
the CGT itself: in early August 1914, after Jaurès's assassination,
the CGT joined the Sacred Union.[3] From that point on, it never
once denounced the nationalist butchery of the First World
War, even though it had still been fiercely opposed to the war
in late July 1914, and had reaffirmed its antiwar position in 1912
and 1913. Rather than go against the prevailing ideas, the union
leadership rushed headlong into the collective patriotic fervor
encouraged by the government. Within the union itself, there
were few who dared to raise their voices against this political
about-face in favor of the war (of which the speech by syndicalist Léon Jouhaux—who was nevertheless their friend—at
Jaurès's funeral marked the prelude).[4]

Though greatly shaken by this abrupt change of course,
Monatte did not give in. He was the first trade union leader to
publicly state his opposition to the union's new stance and quit
his position on the executive committee of the CGT. His letter
of resignation, written in late December 1914, is a resound-
ing appeal across the ages that urges us never to succumb to
the deadly, jingoistic sirens of nationalism that set the people
against each other:

> It is this planned war, feared by us, this desired war, pre-
> pared by our nationalist politicians, that the majority of
> the executive committee now imagines as a war of liber-
> ation for Europe, a war capable of bringing liberty and
> democracy to Germany, and of bringing an end to global
> militarism. What an illusion! The conscious workers
> of the belligerent nations cannot accept the slightest
> responsibility for this war; that weight is entirely on
> the shoulders of the leaders of their countries. And in
> that fact, far from finding reason to draw closer to their
> leaders, they can only renew their hatred for capitalism
> and the state.... If humanity is to one day know peace

and freedom, within the United States of the World, only a more real and more passionate socialism, arising from the present disillusionments, tempered in the rivers of blood that are flowing today, will be able to lead it there. In any case, it will not be the work of the allied armies, nor of the old discredited organizations. It is because I believe, dear comrades, that the CGT has discredited itself that I resign, not without sadness, from the elected post to which you have entrusted me.[5]

In essence, Monatte was one of the first high-profile public figures in France to side with internationalism against the war. In his *Souvenirs*, he explains:

It was a staggering blow to me. I needed to ruminate and to sit with my despair. The ground had collapsed beneath my feet.... Astonishment before the explosion of jingoism within the working class. Even more so before the derailment of so many anarchist and union militants, of almost all the socialists. Had socialism just been killed? Had the war swept away our class consciousness, our hope for the emancipation of the workers of all countries? ... It was difficult not to believe that our ideas of only yesterday were anything more than lamentable ruins. You had to hang on, to hold out, as painful as it was.[6]

In 1917, the Russian Revolution gave him hope again and drew him toward the communist experiment. He saw, in the international excitement about the revolution, the possibility of rekindling the class struggle in France. In his letter to Trotsky in March 1920, he wrote: "The French working class will soon rediscover its revolutionary spirit. Our ideas, today like yesterday, rest upon yours. You fight for yourself and for us. We fight for you and ourselves, ashamed to have not done more and for still being so weak. But better days will come.

They are coming. Your triumph prepares and announces ours."[7]

This letter never reached its destination. Instead, it fell into the hands of the French police, and earned Monatte several months in prison on grounds of conspiring against the security of the state. The tale of this lost letter is a bit like the missed connection between the early revolutionary trade unionists and the birth of the Communist Party in France—a connection in which Trotsky, who saw "revolutionary syndicalism as the only truly revolutionary force," placed much of his hope for France. In exile, Trotsky stayed in Paris and Sèvres from November 1914 before being arrested by the police and expelled into Spain in October 1916, where he didn't stay long—in early 1917 he was sent by force to the United States. After his two years in France, where he had gotten to know the revolutionary trade-unionist milieu, he put himself to work trying to convince the historical leadership of the CGT to take active participation in founding the party, advising them not to hold onto the policy from syndicalism's origins—independence from political parties. It was a policy ill suited, according to him, to respond to the strategic stakes set up by the Russian Revolution. He suggested they make their position clear in a postface to the Charter of Amiens. Although Rosmer signed onto this takeover, and readily got involved, Monatte, for his part, preferred to keep a syndicalist approach to politics. The reason he remained fiercely opposed to the trade-unionist schism in France, for example, even though he was convinced of the need to join the Profintern when it was founded in 1921: the Comintern.[8] For that same reason, he hesitated to enter the French Communist Party for a long time. He did not join until 1923, even though he had felt irresistibly drawn to communist ideals since 1917. However, he barely stayed for a year. Disgusted by the rampant bureaucratization of the party, he was expelled in November 1924. He, Rosmer, and Victor Delagarde signed a text that ended with the words: "What is important is not that we may be struck with expulsion from the Party, but that under the label of Bolshevization, they are exacerbating the latest autocratic methods which are surely the most blatant repudiation of both Bolshevism and communism."[9]

From 1925 on, Pierre Monatte continued his struggle through a new journal, *Révolution prolétarienne*. An indefatigable opponent of reformism and Stalinism until the end of his life, he never abandoned his union activity, nor forgot to regularly reaffirm his internationalism, notably during the anticolonial struggles in Tunisia and Indochina in the early 1950s.

Monatte and Rosmer's momentum ran up against two of the great tragedies of the early twentieth century: the nationalism of World War I and the Stalinist counterrevolution. Yet in the gaps between these two monstrous obstacles, the two men nevertheless managed to blaze a narrow path, an indelible trail that leads us back to them.

Monatte was a red and black luminary who cannot be categorized. The most Marxist of the libertaires before the war became, in a way, the most libertaire of the Marxists after the first global conflict. For his part, he preferred to define himself as a "communist syndicalist."

Rosa Luxemburg (1870–1919)

Rosa Luxemburg, the renowned Polish-German Jewish revolutionary, was assassinated in January 1919 by paramilitary groups mobilized by the Social Democratic government against the workers of Berlin. She was never an anarchist, and in her writings we find many criticisms of anarchist ideas; she always remained committed to the Marxist conception of the party as the political manifestation of the working class. But due to certain aspects of her thought and her revolutionary action, we consider her as being close to a libertaire culture: her critique of the bureaucratic authoritarianism at the heart of the workers' movement, her antimilitarism, her antinationalism, her confidence in the spontaneity of the masses, her insistence on a proletarian revolution from below, and her passionate defense of individual and collective freedoms are elements of this latent affinity. It is no coincidence that one of the most prominent thinkers of libertarian socialism, Daniel Guérin, devoted a book to the subject, *Rosa Luxemburg et la spontanéité révolutionnaire* (1971; Rosa Luxemburg and revolutionary spontaneity).

As a Polish labor activist in the czarist Russian Empire, she criticized early on the tendencies of the Bolsheviks that she found too authoritarian and too centralized. Refuting, in a 1904 article, the idea shared by Karl Kautsky and Lenin of a socialist consciousness introduced to the working class "from

Figure 4. Rosa Luxemburg. © Photothèque Hachette.

outside," she proposed a dialectical conception of the relation between consciousness and struggle: "The proletarian army is recruited and becomes aware of its objectives in the course of the struggle itself. The activity of the party organization, the growth of the proletarians' awareness of the objectives of the struggle and the struggle itself, are not different things separated chronologically and mechanically. They are only different aspects of the same process."[1]

Of course, Rosa Luxemburg recognized, the working class might make mistakes in the course of this fight, but in her final analysis, "Historically, the errors committed by a truly revolutionary movement are infinitely more fruitful than the infallibility of the cleverest Central Committee."[2] The self-emancipation of the oppressed implies the self-transformation of the revolutionary working class by its practical experience. For Lenin, editor of the newspaper *Iskra*, the revolutionary "spark" is brought by the organized political vanguard from the outside to the inside of the spontaneous struggles of the proletariat; for Luxemburg, the revolutionary Polish Jew, the spark of consciousness and revolutionary spirit will itself flare up in the struggle, in the action of the masses. This image demonstrates the divergence of ideas between Rosa Luxemburg and the Lenin of 1903.

The revolutionary events of 1905 in czarist Russia largely confirmed Rosa Luxemburg in her conviction that the making of a working-class consciousness results from direct action and the autonomy of the workers. As she writes in *The Mass Strike, the Political Party, and the Trade Unions* (1906), "Absolutism in Russia must be overthrown by the proletariat. But in order to be able to overthrow it, the proletariat requires a high degree of political education, of class-consciousness and organisation. All these conditions cannot be fulfilled by pamphlets and leaflets, but only by the living political school, by the fight and in the fight, in the continuous course of the revolution."[3]

Her conception of the striking masses differs from that of the anarchists, but the similarities are evident, as Karl Kautsky (1854–1938), Engels's former secretary who became an important leader within the Social Democratic Party of Germany, soon denounced. In a 1913 polemic titled *Der Politische Massenstreik*, Kautsky, who was also the editor of the most important German socialist journal, *Die Neue Zeit*, which he founded in 1883, accused Luxemburg of advancing "anarcho-syndicalist" theses in her 1906 text, and of carrying out "a synthesis of social-democratic and anarchist concepts."[4]

As leader of the left wing of the Social Democratic Party of Germany, Rosa Luxemburg fought against the tendency toward political and union bureaucracy, and the tendency of parliamentary representation to monopolize political decisions. The Russian general strike of 1905 seemed to her an example to follow in Germany as well: she had more confidence in the initiative of the working-class base than in the "wise" decisions of the governing bodies of the German labor movement.

Learning of the events of October 1917 while in prison, Luxemburg immediately declared her solidarity with the Russian revolutionaries. In a pamphlet titled *The Russian Revolution*—which she wrote in prison in 1918 but which was not published until 1921, two years after her death—she pays a warm tribute to the leaders of the October Revolution. But this solidarity did not prevent her from criticizing what seemed erroneous or dangerous in their politics. Noting the impossibility—given the dire circumstances of the civil war and foreign intervention—that the Bolsheviks could "conjure forth the finest democracy" she nevertheless also draws attention to the danger of a slide toward authoritarianism, and insists on the decisive importance of individual and collective liberties in all revolutionary processes:

> Freedom only for the supporters of the government, only for the members of one party—however numerous they may be—is no freedom at all. Freedom is always and exclusively freedom for the one who thinks differently.... Without general elections, without unrestricted freedom of press and assembly, without a free struggle of opinion, life dies out in every public institution, becomes a mere semblance of life, in which only the bureaucracy remains as the active element. [Socialism is] a historical product, born out of the school of its own experiences.[5]

The whole of the working-class masses must participate in this experience, otherwise "socialism will be decreed from behind a few official desks by a dozen intellectuals."[6]

For the inevitable errors during the transition process, the only remedy is the revolutionary practice itself: "the only healing and purifying sun is the revolution itself and its renovating principle, the spiritual life, activity and initiative of the masses which is called into being by it and which takes the form of the broadest political freedom."[7] This argument is much more important than the controversy that was born from the chapter she devoted in *The Russian Revolution* to "the dissolution of the Constituent Assembly," upon which the "Leninist" objections were concentrated.[8]

Without democratic freedoms, the revolutionary praxis of the masses, the working-class's self-education by experience, the self-emancipation of the oppressed, and the exercise of power itself by the laboring class are impossible.

It is difficult not to recognize the prophetic significance of Rosa Luxemburg's warning. A few years later, bureaucracy would take over the totality of the government in the Soviet Union, gradually eliminating the October revolutionaries. During the 1930s, the extermination of all presumed opponents would be merciless.

In one of her final speeches, during the establishment of the German Communist Party (the Spartacus League) in January 1919, Rosa Luxemburg explained her conception of seizing power: contrary to bourgeois revolutions, which limit themselves to overthrowing the official power, and replacing it with a few new men, the proletarian revolution must "build from below upwards.... We must effect the conquest of political power, not from above, but from beneath."[9] Her criticism this time was directed against the Social Democratic Party of Germany, which was then limiting itself to installing its men at the head of the bourgeois state.

Emma Goldman (1869–1940)

A brilliant author and tireless agitator, the Russian-American Jewish anarchist Emma Goldman is one of the most fascinating figures of libertarian socialism in the twentieth century. Born in 1869 in Lithuania (at the time a province of the czarist Russian Empire), she emigrated to the United States at the age of fifteen. Captivated by the trial and execution of the Haymarket Martyrs in Chicago in 1887, she began exploring anarchist ideas. She soon became the friend and lover of a Russian Jewish anarchist living in New York, Alexander ("Sasha") Berkman. Together, they planned the assassination of the heavy-handed steel magnate Henry Clay Frick, who had forcibly broken up striking steelworkers with the help of the Pinkerton private detective agency. Emma tried to work as a prostitute to acquire the money necessary to buy Berkman a revolver with which to shoot Frick—an episode that inspired Jorge Luis Borges to write one of his most remarkable tales, "Emma Zunz." The attack was carried out, but Frick survived his wounds. Sasha Berkman was sentenced to twenty-two years in prison. In 1901, Emma, too, was jailed, wrongfully accused of having ties to Leon Czolgosz, the anarchist who assassinated President William McKinley. Goldman had, in fact, already turned away from the tactic of individual acts of "propaganda by the deed" to focus instead on spoken and written anarchist propaganda. In 1906, after Berkman's release, he joined her

Figure 5. Emma Goldman at the age of seventeen, in 1886.
© Photothèque Hachette.

in founding the famous anarchist magazine *Mother Earth*. In the years that followed, she traveled throughout the country, courageously delivering speeches in defense of contraception, free love, and anarchism, and against patriotism and militarism. Neither Marx nor Bakunin, but rather Peter Kropotkin and Johann Most—a German anarchist who had emigrated to the United States in 1882, after having served time in prison in Germany for praising the assassination of Czar Alexander II—were among her principal references.

Nicknamed "Red Emma" by the press, she was jailed or imprisoned several more times throughout her life. After she denounced World War I and conscription, she spent two years in prison before being deported to Russia in 1919, along with Alexander Berkman and other radicals. A young J. Edgar Hoover, the fanatical reactionary on the eve of his rapid ascension within what would become the FBI, personally oversaw her expulsion from the country, declaring her "the most dangerous woman in America."[1]

Like many anarchists, Emma and Sasha were inspired by the 1917 October Revolution and supported the Bolsheviks from their arrival in the USSR in January 1920. They struck up friendships with their Marxist communist comrades, and shared an apartment with their old New York friends, the American communists John Reed and Louise Bryant. For a time after their arrival, the American anarchists still enjoyed a certain liberty: they published newspapers and held conferences. Emma spoke with Karl Radek, Alexandra Kollontai, Angelica Balabanoff, Victor Serge, and others. She and Sasha were received by Lenin, who expressed his great admiration for them, and compared them to Malatesta, who, according to Lenin, was "entirely with Soviet Russia." "What is it you prefer to do?" he asked them. The two proposed the creation of a support committee for radical struggles in America, and Lenin was delighted with this "brilliant idea." The exchange is described in detail by Emma Goldman in her memoirs.[2]

During their conversation, and many times over the two years that followed, Emma and Sasha fought to secure the liberation of Russian anarchists imprisoned by the Bolsheviks, often with success—for example, in the case of Voline.[3] They were also charged with collecting documents for the creation of a museum of the revolution, a task to which they passionately devoted themselves; at that time, they still considered themselves loyal—though critical—partisans of the USSR. Emma was also soon charged, along with Angelica Balabanoff, with receiving the British Labour Mission, led by Bertrand Russell, and convincing them of the benefits of the Russian Revolution.

Despite it all, Emma Goldman and Alexander Berkman were more and more disappointed by the authoritarianism of Bolshevik officials, the arbitrary arrests, the omnipotence of the Cheka, and the growing repression carried out against the anarchists. Kropotkin's funeral in February 1921 was the last occasion for a massive public demonstration of anarchist opinion in the USSR.

The breaking point came with the uprising of the sailors and workers at Kronstadt, and the crackdown that followed. Shortly before the Red Army advanced on the rebels, Emma and Sasha sent an urgent appeal to Zinoviev, titular member of the Politburo: "The use of force.... against the workers and sailors [of Kronstadt]," they wrote, would "result in incalculable harm to the Social Revolution," not only in Russia, but throughout the world. "Comrades Bolsheviki, bethink yourselves before it is too late."[4] Their appeal was made in vain.

In late 1921, Emma and Sasha were granted visas by the Soviet authorities to attend an anarchist congress in Berlin and used the opportunity to leave the USSR for good. And so ended an emblematic episode of the convergence between anarchists and Communists in the first years after the October Revolution. Emma Goldman published *My Disillusionment in Russia* a few years later, which bitterly summed up her personal experience.

Goldman found refuge first in Germany and then in England. She traveled to Spain several times between 1936 and 1938 to support the revolutionary antifascist fight of the National Confederation of Labor–Iberian Anarchist Federation. In her writings, she denounced the detrimental role of the Stalinist communists and Soviet agents, especially during the show trial of the leadership of the Workers' Party of Marxist Unification (POUM). "I do not agree with the ideology of the POUM. It is a Marxist party and I have been and am absolutely opposed to Marxism," she wrote in 1938, "but that cannot prevent me from paying respects to the mentality and courage of Gorkin, Andrade, and their comrades. Their stand in court was magnificent. Their exposition of their ideas was clear cut. There were no evasions or apologies. In point of fact the seven men in the dock demonstrated, for the first time since the demoralization of all idealists in Russia, how revolutionists should face their accusers."[5]

Emma Goldman died in Canada in 1940 and is buried in Chicago near the graves of the anarcho-syndicalist Haymarket Martyrs. Her memory and her example are celebrated by Marxists and anarchists alike. The historian Howard Zinn, author of *A People's History of the United States* and the play *Marx in Soho*, also wrote a play simply entitled *Emma*.

Buenaventura Durruti (1896–1936)

Durruti was an anarchist, and a libertaire militant during the Spanish Revolution. While it might seem difficult at first glance to find any overlap between his politics and Marxism, many Marxists, in fact, hold him in very high regard. Indeed, Durruti's exceptional accomplishments, his ideas, and his actions remain a reference for all those who, beyond dogma, red or black, seek to unify theory and practice. In his book *Durruti in the Spanish Revolution*, Abel Paz tells the epic, fantastic story of his life.[1]

Born in 1896, he grew up at a time when Spain, shaken by the loss of its last colonial possessions, was stricken by regular revolts in a climate of social strife. From a very young age, he felt "intuitively, [that he] had already become a rebel," as he later wrote to his sister Rosa.[2] In the León region where his family lived there were repeated strikes, in which his father participated, and which were severely suppressed; this set the scene for the young Durruti's radicalization. A metalworker from the age of fourteen, he took part in political and union struggles, and soon turned to the revolutionary trade-unionist camp of the already-powerful Confederación Nacional del Trabajo (CNT; National Confederation of Labor), as socialist theorists were too moderate in his eyes. So began an extraordinary political saga.

Durruti was a militant who was brought to the forefront out of anonymity by the events of his time. For though he

Figure 6. Buenaventura Durruti, graphic by Maurici Bellmunt. Reproduced by permission from Jaume Nolla and Margarita Puig, *Muertos ilustres en los cementerios de Barcelona: Todo lo que hay que saber de los que nos han precedido* (Barcelona: Angle Editorial, 2007).

was a man of his time, forged by intense class struggles, he was also an atypical young man. Laid off in the wake of the general strike of August 1917, caught in the grip of a crack-down, Durruti and other syndicalists began to take more radical action. He deserted the army and lived on the run, first underground and then in exile, and began pulling off daring feats as he went.[3] Many young men, Durruti included, faced with repressive violence from the bosses, arbitrary harass-ment, and systematic arrests, decided to organize themselves into small, determined anarchist groups, acting beyond the boundaries of normal union activity. For Durruti, this mostly meant robbing banks to finance the union, and engaging in armed resistance against the *pistoleros*, the militias backed by the bosses—these were his main activities for nearly five years, until 1922.

The political tension came to a head in 1923: in the wake of the military coup d'état in Barcelona on September 13, the new dictatorial regime began trying to stifle the revolutionary momentum that had been rising since 1917. The bosses' militias began blindly and systematically cracking down on anarchist activists. Durruti's life tipped over from armed resistance into armed struggle. His affinity group, Los Solidarios, decided to take out a number of public figures in retaliation: several *pistoleros*, José Regueral (the former governor of Bilbao), and Juan Soldevila (the Archbishop of Saragossa) were their targets. The Primo de Rivera regime, against which attempts at armed struggle regularly failed, soon set its sights on Los Solidarios, and Durruti left Spain for Latin America in December 1924. His life in Cuba and Argentina was a mix of guerrilla warfare, odd jobs, assassinations, union organizing, and bank robbery. If it were a Hollywood screenplay, it would probably be rejected as too unrealistic. Yet it is true.

His journey continued. In France, in April 1926, he was arrested for plotting to assassinate the king of Spain, Alfonso XIII. Upon his release from prison, he traveled clandestinely around Europe, including France, Belgium, and Germany. On the Iberian Peninsula, large-scale social movements began to breathe new life into the union movement from 1929.

With the fall of the Primo de Rivera regime in 1930 and then the advent of the Republic in April 1931, Durruti made up his mind: he was going home. So began his second life, more focused on activism and radical, revolutionary trade union-ism but just as focused on mass public actions, and therefore in close touch with the real forces of Spanish society. The anarchist "adventurer" was still an anarchist, but he now gave a visible libertaire political dimension to his action. Los Solidarios, until then an armed group, became an activist nucleus that played a prominent role in the revolutionary process up until 1936.

The failure of the moderate Republican camp in its relentless repression of the CNT in 1931 served only to strengthen the latter's prestige. The anarchist organizations regrouped within the CNT, creating the Federación Anarquista Ibérica (FAI; Iberian Anarchist Federation), in which Durruti was an active and influential organizer. He spent several stretches in the jails of the Republic between 1931 and 1936. His imprisonment in 1931, several months long, only reinforced his political convictions. His analysis began to take shape, galvanized by a prerevolutionary context that forced radical activists like him to face the full extent of their responsibilities. When the Republican Left government ended its term discredited by its experiment with power, the inevitable return of the Far Right in November 1933, combined with a major economic crisis, created a tense and polarized situation. At the bottom of society, it was explosive. Seen from above, it became uncontrollable. The failed insurrections of December 1933, then January 1934, did nothing to reverse the current of radicalization simmering throughout Spain. The election of the Popular Front in February 1936 was the natural trigger point of the revolutionary process. Grown strong by their experiences in recent years, the masses burst spectacularly onto the political scene.

It was then that Durruti showed himself to be an excellent organizer. It was his view that the revolution could not be reduced to abstract political ideas: those ideas were given life by their collective practical application, and in the collective process of learning from them. This pragmatism allowed his ideas to evolve in close contact with the social realities that the CNT inevitably had to address. The CNT, at this time, numbered more than 1.5 million members, giving it a pivotal role in the labor movement. According to Durruti, the only way to keep the movement going was by comparing its ideals with what was actually going on in the world of labor—which served as a good antidote against dogmatism as well.

Having himself left behind individual action in favor of collective struggle, Durruti reflected on his own path. He believed in the emancipatory power of class struggle, but he also believed in the importance of the role of the organization in carrying out the revolution. His encounter with the Ukrainian revolutionary anarchist Nestor Makhno during his exile in Paris, in 1927, probably strengthened this belief in him. It was a question of being effective against the powers in place. It was anarchism's duty to be a system of thought in perpetual motion, to call itself into question and perfect itself through the experiences it accumulated as it went along. And so, in 1933, as the moment of revolution, which he foresaw was imminent, drew near, Durruti wasted no time in condemning the individual acts of banditry carried out in the name of anarchism.[4]

From then on, it was the time for collective, rather than individual, expropriation. It was the circumstances of the real world that guided the actions of the revolutionaries. Anarchism had evolved, passed through an embryonic phase where the circulation of ideas was reserved for a small, politically conscious minority, to a higher level that had to take into account the complexity of the relations between social and political forces. Yet Durruti's pragmatism never took him away from his profound convictions. "Durruti's great secret was that he made theory and practice into one thing," Emma Goldman once said of him.[5]

Durruti considered political questions in an original way within the libertaire movement. No longer ignoring the reality of the government in power did not mean, for him, succumbing to its charms, nor seeking to substitute it with another form of oppression. Questions of political power were to be asked, but they needed to be considered in a revolutionary perspective: "Those who say we wanted to take over and impose a dictatorship are liars. Our revolutionary convictions repudiate such a goal. We want a revolution for the people and by the people, because proletarian liberation is impossible otherwise.... We are neither Blanquists nor Trotskyists, but understand that this journey is long and that it has to be made *by moving, by going forward.*"[6]

At the same time, the CNT's exact stance on politics was in flux. The leadership's position moved from one of electoral abstentionism—typical among the anarchists in 1933—to one of governmental integration, working alongside the bourgeois Republican forces in 1936 and 1937. Four libertaires became ministers in the Republican government. Durruti, for his part, sought a middle path between political impotence and opportunism, without necessarily finding it.

It was more by intuition than by theorizing that he decided not to approve of the CNT's "governmental" direction. He was not delicate with his friends: "You trust the politicians and this makes sense because in associating with them you have become like them, and you believe their promises."[7] He preferred fighting alongside his comrades in the column that bore his name, battling against fascism and spreading the message of the revolution in the wake of his advance.

An anarchist at the head of a column of militiamen and -women might seem paradoxical to some. Durruti was one of those who attempted, on the scale of the revolutionary antifascist militias, to combine two different elements: the discipline necessary for all military endeavors, and the principles of democratic organization. "We'll show you Bolsheviks, both Russian and Spanish, how to have a revolution and how to carry it through. Over there you have a dictatorship, in your army there are colonels and generals. In my column there are neither commanders nor subordinates, we all have the same rights, we're all soldiers, I too am just a soldier."[8] Read today, this statement can seem almost cartoonish in its idealism. It should also be read with skepticism, as the person who reported it did not have Durruti's interests at heart—*Pravda* reporter Mikhail Koltsov was also a Russian agent. Yet behind these words there is an assumed profession of faith: the wish to maintain an alternative to the "militarization" of the militias then being orchestrated by the Republican government.

Under the aegis of the Stalinists, who were more and more active within its ranks, the Republican government decided to disarm and dissolve the people's militias, beginning in late summer 1936. Only the People's Republican Army would now exist; it began to institute this army, based on a hierarchical model and dominated by the men from Moscow. The disarmament of the anarchist militias and of the POUM was the decisive blow of the Spanish counterrevolution.

Yet nothing could erase the fact that the Durruti Column had heroically fought back the Francoists, and in so doing proved that military efficiency was not an argument for authoritarian discipline in and of itself. The experiment in democratically organized armed forces is a complex one, but not impossible. The long time needed for debate coincides poorly with the short time needed for prompt military decisions. That said, the flag that flew over the column was very much red and black.

Durruti explained:

> I don't believe ... that you can run a workers' militia according to classical military rules. I believe that discipline, coordination, and planning are indispensable, but we shouldn't define them in the terms of the world that we're destroying.... My comrades and I are convinced that solidarity is the best incentive for arousing individual responsibility and a willingness to accept discipline as an act of self-discipline.... The combatant is nothing more than a worker whose tool is a rifle—and he should strive toward the same objective as the worker. One can't behave like an obedient soldier, but as a conscious man

who understands the importance of what he's doing.... I know that it's not easy to achieve this, but I also know that what can't be accomplished with reason will not be obtained by force. If we have to sustain our military apparatus with fear, then we won't have changed anything except the color of the fear. It's only by freeing itself from fear that society can build itself in freedom.[9]

A popular and essential figure of the CNT, Durruti is, along with Andreu Nin, one of the two great names of the Spanish Revolution to be betrayed by Stalinism. Trotsky, who felt no particular affection for the Spanish anarchists, nonetheless recognized the CNT as the main revolutionary force where the most combative elements of the proletariat had gathered. More surprising still, in 1937 he made a distinction between Durruti and the rest of the CNT leadership, whom he judged harshly, and compared Nin's assassination with Durruti's death: "Why does every approach to our views or our methods of action (Durruti, Andres Nin....) compel the Stalinist gangsters to resort to bloody reprisals?"[10]

This "proximity" has been celebrated by many revolutionary Marxists over the generations. Such is the case, for example, with our comrades in the Izquierda Anticapitalista (Anticapitalist Left), who are actively bringing life to the ideas of the Fourth International in Spain today; their website refers liberally to Durruti, including his famous quote, "We carry a new world here, in our hearts."

Durruti died in Madrid on November 20, 1936, likely from a stray bullet, in circumstances that remain unexplained. He left a singular mark on the anarchist struggle. It is perhaps for this singularity that, far beyond his immediate political family, many revolutionaries still draw great inspiration from his experience.

Benjamin Péret (1899–1959)

Surrealist poet, revolutionary leftist Benjamin Péret was one of the founders, along with André Breton, of the surrealist movement. Breton described him as "one of the most stubborn against all concessions."[1] Having joined the French Communist Party in 1926, Péret quickly found himself—by 1928—in the Trotskyist Left Opposition. In 1929, he traveled to Brazil with his wife, Elsie Houston, and lived there, organizing with the Brazilian Trotskyists until his expulsion from the country in 1931—he was described as an "agitator," "harmful to the public peace."

Paul Éluard, in 1934, described his poetry as "specifically subversive," having "[the] color of the future." In 1936, having learned of the July 18 uprising in Spain, he left for Barcelona as a delegate for the International Secretariat of the Movement for the Fourth International. He enlisted as a volunteer to fight fascism, first in the ranks of the Workers' Party of Marxist Unification (POUM) militias and then in the Durruti Column. He wrote, succinctly, in a letter to André Breton, "I decided to join an anarchist militia and I'm here on the front. (Durruti Division, Pina del Ebro, Frente de Aragón, 7 March 1937)."

Arrested by the Vichy authorities in 1940, he went into voluntary exile in Mexico for the duration of the war. Upon his return to Paris in 1948, he (along with Natalia Trotsky) broke with the Fourth International, refusing to continue to consider the USSR a "workers' state." In the early 1950s, like several other surrealists, he wrote in *Le Libertaire,* the anarchist periodical run by Georges Fontenis. He remained loyal to surrealism and to revolutionary Marxist ideas until his death in 1959.

I had the good fortune to meet Benjamin Péret once, passing through Paris in 1958—I was bringing him some mail from his friends in Brazil. Having read several of his collections of poetry and being familiar with his political career, I admired him enormously and was very much looking forward to meeting him. We met three or four times, and during one of these encounters, he took me to the local POUM office in Paris, where he introduced me to Wilebaldo Solano, the general secretary. From the beginning, the war and the revolution in Spain were among the principal topics of our conversation. I asked him, with a certain naivety, "So, you left for Spain to fight fascism in the ranks of the International Brigades?"

"Not at all!" he replied, "The Stalinists would've liquidated me with a bullet in the back right away! I joined the Durruti Column, the people from the CNT FAI [National Confederation of Labor–Iberian Anarchist Federation] who were the real revolutionaries." I think that his choice of the Durruti Column was no accident and testified to a sympathy for—and an attraction to—the most uncompromising libertaires on his part. He was also close to them in his fervent antimilitarism, antipatriotism, and anticlericalism. His libertaire affinities are noticeable in his famous collection of poems, *Je ne mange pas de ce pain-là* (I don't eat that bread), published in 1936, among other works.

Péret was not an anarchist—he sometimes debated them fiercely—but he was nonetheless a sort of libertarian Marxist. Another vivid example: his 1955 essay titled "Quilombo de Palmares," a history of the maroon community that resisted the incursions of Portuguese slavers for a hundred years. He interprets this history as a manifestation of the irrepressible desire for freedom. The essay opens with the line: "Of all the sentiments stirring in man's heart, the desire for freedom is surely one of the most compelling." Freedom constitutes "for the mind as for the heart, the oxygen without which it cannot survive. If the physical being cannot live without air, the emotional being can only wither and deteriorate without freedom." It is for this reason that the desire for freedom must accept no concession, no limit, no compromise: "Man's only fault is his pusillanimity. His thirst for freedom will never be too great." These pointed words are pure Benjamin Péret, a man of proud mind and straight back.

When the human being finds itself deprived of freedom, "he has no peace until he wins it back; so much that all of history could be limited to the study of the attacks against this freedom, and the efforts of the oppressed to shake off the yoke that has been imposed on them." Here, Péret reinterprets the "classic" Marxist thesis from a new angle: class struggle as the struggle of the exploited against the exploiters. The history of humanity is that of the continuous struggle of the oppressed for their liberation. And there an entire anthropology of freedom can be found.

Michael Löwy

Subcomandante Marcos (1957–)

Wielding the pen as readily as the gun, Subcomandante Marcos, the widely recognized spokesperson for the Zapatista uprising that began in Mexico in 1994, has invented a new type of language. It is a language that is thankfully distinct from the hollow—if not empty—language of so many political groups. Saturated with humor and even self-deprecation, his writings link together poems, Indigenous myths, children's tales, incendiary proclamations, and threats against the wealthy. From Mayan deities to the short stories of Jorge Luis Borges, from conversations with a scarab to Shakespeare's sonnets, from scenes from Don Quixote to events from Mexican history, he often ends his texts with a challenge, such as: "Zapata is still here, alive and well. Go ahead, try to assassinate him again."[1] It is difficult to escape the bewitching charm of his letter-poem-tracts.

Subcomandante (sub-commander) is an ironic title, and one he assigned to himself to indicate his submission to the Indigenous commanders of the Ejército Zapatista de Liberación Nacional (Zapatista Army of National Liberation), or EZLN— although one might legitimately wonder about the dangers of glorifying any one personality within the movement. Mexico has a strong anarchist tradition, most famously embodied by the Flores Magón brothers, contemporaries of Emiliano Zapata during the Mexican Revolution of 1911–17. Zapata was no anarchist, but he often elicits sympathy from libertaires by his refusal, along with Pancho Villa, to seize power during their victorious occupation of Mexico City in 1914.

Subcomandante Marcos did not come out of this libertaire matrix. He was one of the founders of the National Liberation Forces (FLN), a Guevarist armed organization created in Monterrey, in northern Mexico, in 1969. According to its 1980 statutes, the FLN was a "politico-military organization whose objective is the seizure of political power.... In order to establish a People's Republic and a socialist economic system."[2] It was from the fusion of this first core group and a group of Indigenous combatants in Chiapas that the EZLN was created in 1983. The movement's evolution has carried it quite far from its origins. Nevertheless, the January 1994 uprising, like the spirit itself of the EZLN, has kept some aspects of their heritage intact: the importance of armed struggle, the organic links between the combatants and the peasantry, the gun as the material expression of the distrust of the exploited toward their oppressors, and the readiness to risk one's life for the emancipation of one's brothers and sisters. Though the time and place are far removed from Guevara's 1967 Bolivian expedition, there remain traces of the revolutionary ethic that lead directly back to Che.

It is these characteristics that attract the sympathies of Marxists as well as anarchists, who organized (mostly during the 1990s) support committees for the EZLN in numerous countries. But there are also other traits specific to the Zapatistas, interesting and very new: a revolutionary armed force that does not practice gun worship, an insurgent movement that does not want to seize power, a political organization that rejects the rules of the political game, and a vanguard that doesn't always know where it's going, and doesn't hesitate to confess its hesitation.

In February 1994, when asked about the uprising's objectives, Marcos responded: "Seizing power? No, something a bit more difficult: a new world."[3] To avoid misunderstandings

—such as those that arose in the wake of John Holloway's book *Change the World without Taking Power*, which was intended as a reflection on that Zapatista slogan—allow us to add this: In refusing the seizure of power, the EZLN is breaking with a certain revolutionary model, where the vanguard party— or the liberation army—seizes and monopolizes power in the name of the people. This does *not* mean that the organization does not aspire to a profound, democratic and revolutionary transformation of power, in which it would be taken from the hands of the representatives of capital, both national and global, and placed instead in the hands of the people, the oppressed, the excluded.

The observations of Jérôme Baschet—a brilliant French historian living in Chiapas and known for his close relationship with the Zapatistas—would seem to be pertinent here:

> When the Zapatistas speak of refusing to take power, it must be understood that this means giving up the struggle, as much military as it is political, for *state power*.... The creation of autonomous municipalities by the Zapatistas—which, it cannot be denied, make up a strongly structured form of government—clearly establishes that the Zapatistas are concerned with building new structures of *political power*. If this does not contradict their refusal to seize power, it is because it is a matter, for them, of building this new power from below, and avoiding the trap already perceived by Marx after the experience of the Paris Commune.

Not "taking possession of the apparatus of the state," then, but rather destroying it. Of course, Baschet recognizes that some contradictions do exist within the EZLN, notably between the horizontality of the community and the verticality of the military.[4]

The libertaire aspects of the EZLN—the refusal of state power and electoral/parliamentary politics, a horizontal, bottom-up political structure, antiauthoritarianism (such as in the practice of "leading by obeying"), fighting for local autonomy and the self-government of society against the centralized state—come also in large part from the communal traditions of the Indigenous Maya of Chiapas. They have been combined with the long experience of rebellion and with points of reference from the anarchist tradition. These aspects explain why so many libertaires around the world identify with and support the struggle of the EZLN.

Marcos's speeches, and often the written documents of the Zapatistas as well, largely use a Marxist, anticapitalist, and anti-imperialist vocabulary. But if you look for references to Marx or Marxism, or even Bakunin or anarchism, you will search in vain. The Zapatistas do not like doctrinaire definitions, no matter where they may come from.

II

Points of Conflict

The Russian Revolution (1917–20)

Marxists and anarchists are bound by their common origin. A list of their historical disputes would also have them opposed to one another, an impenetrable jumble of shared references and glaring discords. At the top of this list would necessarily figure the Russian Revolution of 1917. Initially, there was a convergence between many anarchists—not only Russian but also from around the world—and the Marxist revolutionaries. Soon after, the convergence had become a dramatic clash between the two, which reached its peak with Kronstadt and the war against Makhno.

October 1917

In October 1917, the Bolsheviks, having realized their own strength, supplanted the Provisional Government and seized power. The leading figures in this story are the oppressed and exploited masses. Leon Trotsky, in his two volumes devoted to the Bolshevik Revolution, recounts the inexorable rise in the people's power and draws the conclusion: "The most indubitable feature of a revolution is the direct interference of the masses in historical events…. The history of a revolution is for us first of all a history of the forcible entrance of the masses into the realm of rulership over their own destiny."[1] The French anarchist Daniel Guérin (1904–1988) saw the same thing: "The Russian Revolution was, in fact, a great mass movement, a wave rising from the people which passed over and submerged ideological formations. It belonged to no one, unless to the people."[2] Both of them, each in his own way, offer a similar appreciation of what the revolution gave rise to in and of itself—though they are far from agreement on the totality of 1917.

The October Revolution was the result of the movement that began in February which, by its dynamic, pulled the masses ever further to the left. There was nothing mechanical or linear about it. The process occurred in fits and starts, evolving with the ebb and flow of revolutionary outbursts and reactionary counteroffensives. In fact, the February Revolution held the seeds of the October Revolution—one brought on the other. Over the course of those eight months, the masses had gotten their first taste of governing with Alexander Kerensky's Provisional Government, which had become an obstacle to their emancipation. Coalitions were made and unmade, caught in the clutches of a duality of power that had become unworkable, perpetually forced to choose between the authority of the Duma (the representatives of the moderate Left and the Socialist-Revolutionaries), and that of the Petrograd Soviet (the representatives of the communist workers in Petrograd). It was in this context that the insurrection organized by the Bolsheviks handed power over to the Second All-Russian Congress of Soviets on October 25, 1917.

It was then that the discord between Marxists and libertaires began. It has to do with the thorny problem of the relationship between political parties and the revolutionary process itself. The Bolsheviks, as a political organization, undoubtedly played a decisive role in the revolution, without which the events of October probably would not have occurred. The question is whether this role had a detrimental effect on the movement's ability to self-organize. The facts tend to demonstrate that the soviets grew stronger at the end of the October uprising, with Kerensky's dismissal strengthening their legitimacy. The debate, then, likely lies elsewhere. Daniel

Guérin does not contest this point. The Bolsheviks, at least for the first year of the revolution, worked alongside the spontaneous mass movements, helping them to collectivize the means of production from the outset. In more concrete terms, the implementation of workers' control ran up against resistance from the capitalists, and in this way prompted the Bolsheviks to take increasingly radical steps in the direction of self-management. Guérin explains: "Workers' control soon had to give place to socialization. Lenin literally did violence to his more timorous lieutenants by throwing them into the 'crucible of living popular creativity,' by obliging them to speak in authentic libertarian language. The basis of revolutionary reconstruction was to be workers' self-management."[3]

Guérin dates the end of the Bolsheviks' libertaire period at the spring of 1918, and explains it by the dualism of Marxist ideas about the state, which Lenin summed up in September 1917 in his book *The State and Revolution*.[4] Two extremes, two contradictory concepts cohabitated in Marxist thought: a libertaire version that clearly wanted to abolish the capitalist state, and an authoritarian version that preferred the establishment of a new, Marxist state, which was supposed to fade away on its own, but lived endlessly on. In Guérin's opinion, this ambivalence tends to reappear automatically at the first sign that the popular revolutionary process is losing steam.

The Split between Red and Black

Unlike Guérin, Victor Serge does not see in the rampant bureaucratization an ideological flaw, tied to a possible hidden side of Marxism. He objects, rather, to an error of management—one with heavy consequences—in a context that is particularly complex and difficult to grasp.

At the time that the end of the libertaire period appeared in the spring of 1918, the Russian revolutionary movement was in need of a second wind. Red Finland had been drowned in blood in April 1918 and the Spartacist Uprising in Germany failed in early 1919. The Hungarian Soviet Republic, which emerged in March 1919, was liquidated in August of the same year. In a word, the extension of the revolution to the West was stalling. Internally, the revolutionary front was continually fracturing—a phenomenon whose origin may not necessarily rest with the Bolsheviks.

The Left Socialist-Revolutionaries, who had been participating in the government, disagreed with the Treaty of Brest-Litovsk, which was signed in March 1918.[5] They staged a revolt in Moscow, which failed. De facto, they left the Bolsheviks holding the reins of power alone. The Allies were landing to the north;[6] Japan had seized Vladivostok; Germany had taken Crimea, Ukraine, Estonia, and Lithuania, while the White Army threatened the interior. Despite the Civil War and the uncertainties of the future, the Bolsheviks pressed forward, offering the revolution the possibility of something better. The revolution held out. But from 1920 on, with "war communism" implemented due to the prevailing emergency, necessity began to take over from law.

In "Thirty Years After the Russian Revolution," Victor Serge speaks of the summer of 1920 as a "fatal moment."[7] It is in this same period that he situates the "drama of anarchism, which was to achieve historic significance with the Kronstadt uprising," as he describes in his *Memoirs of a Revolutionary*.[8] With the exception of the Makhnovists' epic in Ukraine between 1917 and 1921, the anarchists, despite all they had contributed, had not been in a real position to influence the course of the revolution.[9] Several emblematic figures of Russian anarchism, such as Kropotkin, had strayed into supporting the war, the army, and even nationalism during World War I, profoundly destabilizing and dividing the anarchist movement.[10]

That being said, up until 1919, many different groups played an active part in the revolution, often conducting their own, autonomous propaganda campaigns within the soviets and businesses. From the earliest days of the revolution, the libertaires championed the Soviet revolution, retaining their independent, critical point of view, and maintaining a contradictory relationship with the Bolsheviks, at once both supportive and confrontational. The same could be said of the Bolsheviks' relationship with the anarchists. In Moscow, for example, over the fall of 1918, after the failed coup d'état by the Left Socialist Revolutionary Party, the Black Guards[11] had not ruled out the possibility of taking over the city, a position that immediately provoked debate and disagreement among the anarchists, particularly in the anarcho-syndicalist group Golos Truda (the Voice of Labor). In 1920, this group was still well established. Emma Goldman recounts her arrival in Moscow that same year:

> Our comrades in Moscow, Sasha informed me, seemed to enjoy considerable freedom. The Anarcho-Syndicalists of the group Golos Truda were publishing anarchist literature and selling it openly at their book-shop on the Tverskaya. The Universalist Anarchists had club-rooms with a co-operative restaurant and held open weekly gatherings at which revolutionary problems were freely discussed.... "What an extraordinary situation!" I remarked, "to grant anarchists in Moscow so much freedom, and none at all to the Petrograd circle!" ... Sasha explained that he had come upon quite a number of strange contradictions. Thus, many of our comrades were in prison, for no cause apparently, while others were not molested in their activities.[12]

Voline was imprisoned in January 1920. Efim Yarchuk, a famous anarchist of the Kronstadt Soviet (*soviet* meaning "workers' council" in Russian) was arrested several times between 1918 and 1921. This policy was the trademark of the arbitrariness that was entering irreversibly into an ever more policed society.

Created in December 1917, the Cheka—a Russian acronym for "All-Russian Extraordinary Commission for Combating Counter-Revolution and Sabotage"—gradually extended its reach at every available opportunity; soon, it saw that its time had come. A political police force, initially empowered to act against the White Guards upon orders only, the Cheka gained a great deal of autonomy and a marked increase in power in the summer of 1918 when it was entrusted with the ability to sentence people it had arrested to death.[13] In January 1920, when the Bolsheviks abolished the death penalty (later reinstated), the Cheka caught the government off guard and executed a large number of prisoners without authorization, thus demonstrating their independence.

The variety of treatments in store for libertaire activists in the newborn Soviet Union was not only a sign of the rampant repression, but also brought forth the divisions running through the anarchist movement at that time. Victor Serge deplored this fracturing: "The anarchists were chaotically subdivided into pro-Soviet, anti-Soviet camps, and intermediate tendencies."[14] One faction entered into active participation within the soviets, even up to the point of working in the governmental commissariats, never forgetting the authority of the Comintern.[15] Lenin, by the way, showed himself to be favorable to this collaboration, at least until the summer of 1920, at the International's Second World Congress. The "universalist" anarchists, for their part, fell somewhat into line. Others were radically opposed to the new power—in September 1919, an anarchist railway man threw a bomb in the middle of a meeting of the Moscow Committee of the Communist Party, killing several people. At the same time, anarchists were participating in the defense of Petrograd against the Whites, side by side with the Bolsheviks on the front lines: "The anarchists were mobilized for the work of defense. The Party gave them arms.... It was they who, on the night of their worst danger, occupied the printing works of *Pravda*, the Bolshevik paper that they hated, ready to defend it to the death."[16]

But beginning in November 1920, tempers became very frayed between the Bolsheviks and the anarchists. The

Bolsheviks seemed to have made up their minds to place the anarchists among the subversive elements of the "internal threat" category. A short time previously, Lev Kamenev, in the name of the Moscow Soviet, had proposed to the anarchists the "legalization of their movement, complete with its own press, clubs, and bookshops, on condition that they should draw up a register of themselves and conduct a purge of their favorite haunts."[17] A condition rejected by the anarchists, and with good reason.

At the very same time in Ukraine, Makhno's Black Army and the Red Army had just won a decisive victory together over the Whites—and then the Bolsheviks brutally broke off the alliance. The crackdown was widespread: "In Petrograd and Moscow the anarchists were making ready for their Congress. But no sooner had this joint victory been won than they were suddenly (in November 1920) arrested en masse by the Cheka. The Black victors of the Crimea, Karetnik, Gavrilenko, and others were betrayed, arrested, and shot.... This fantastic attitude of the Bolshevik authorities, who tore up the pledges they themselves had given to this endlessly daring revolutionary peasant minority, had a terribly demoralizing effect; in it I see one of the basic causes of the Kronstadt rising," wrote Victor Serge.

Party and Soviets

In hindsight, it appears that, between Lenin's "pro-soviet" period and the "war communism" period, a bond was broken, and not only in the treatment of the libertaires. The early policy of self-management had gradually been swept aside under the drastic requirements of the war effort, allowing the bureaucratic wolf in sheep's clothing to enter the fold of the revolution. In 1917 and 1918, Rosa Luxemburg did not hold back from criticizing the absence of political and democratic liberties, the monopolizing role of the party, and the fact that the Constituent Assembly had not been convened. Her protests, however, had not the slightest impact on her loyal support of the Bolshevik revolution. In her view, the guarantee of expression and criticism of events as they actually took place was the best way to encourage the involvement of the working class, and in turn ensure that the revolution survived and thrived. It was no small matter for socialist democracy.

Understood in this light, the key is then to analyze what it was in the Bolsheviks' policies that served as such fertile ground for the Stalinist Thermidor.[18] Did the Bolsheviks take measures that, under the pressure of events of the revolution, paved the way for a nascent bureaucracy? This is an entirely legitimate line of questioning. The Supreme Soviet of the National Economy, for example, played an increasingly important role within the economic administration from 1918 onward, prioritizing centralized nationalization over the local collectivization of the means of production that had been taking place from the beginning. This choice, like so many others, is questionable. It is pointless, however, to seek a manufacturing defect in Marxism and to return to the original ideological disagreement of the First International, when Marx and Bakunin debated each other on the question of whether to abolish the state immediately or not. Reduced to this single aspect, the discussion quickly becomes a dialogue of the deaf. Certainly, Trotsky recognized that "the dangers of state power exist under the regime of the dictatorship of the proletariat as well,"[19] and that "the state, even the workers' state, is the offspring of class barbarism and that real human history will begin with the abolition of the state."[20] But Daniel Guérin criticizes him for not asking the question in these terms instead: "How—in what way, by what methods—to lead to the definitive abolition of the state?"[21] But then, from 1917 onward, the stakes became more immediate and often less abstract than the question and its formulations.

The nagging question that interfered with the Bolsheviks' maneuvering during the events of the revolution is not, in any case, this one, but another question, no less significant: "Who takes power?" Or, more precisely, "Who continues to hold it? The soviets and/or the party/parties?" Libertaires assert that behind this question hides the dilemma of power, and therefore of the state. Of power, yes, though not necessarily that of the state itself, unless we assume that every type of power carries within it the gene for state control—a conviction that many currents of anarchism do indeed hold. On the other hand, for some, self-management and the power of the soviets already constitute a form of power; they are not the *absence* of power. They are akin to that "political form at last discovered" that Marx spoke of regarding the Paris Commune.[22]

In October 1917, the Bolsheviks seem to have let themselves become blinded by an unforeseen optical effect: during the October insurrection, the two entities—soviets and party— were de facto superimposed, one upon the other. The masses were self-radicalizing ever faster—a result of Kornilov's failed coup d'état and the procrastination of the Provisional Government—so much so that the soviets were declaring their allegiance to the Bolsheviks by themselves. When the Bolsheviks' armed offensive deposed the Kerensky government and handed power over to the Congress of Soviets, which was beginning at the same time, the leadership of the party and that of the congress were undeniably the same. This transitory "fusion" may have induced a chronic political squint: Which organization took priority in the long run, in the decision-making process?

The Bolsheviks were unsure on this question. Lenin and Trotsky fluctuated frequently on the subject. Yet Trotsky asserted: "No, the government of the soviets was not a chimera, an arbitrary construction, an invention of party theoreticians. It grew up irresistibly from below."[23] Later, however, he argued that it should be the party that takes power. It is true that in the heat of the moment, and before the dangers of the bureaucratic takeover had made themselves painfully felt, the Bolsheviks did not turn their attention to this risk—a risk they did not anticipate.

Today, the tragic track record of the revolutions of the past century compels us to think otherwise, if we hope to one day return a more human face to the socialist cause. Building antibureaucratic revolutionary organizations is one of the strongest guarantees for any revolution to guard against authoritarian drift. But it is not the only one, for beyond the organizations that a revolutionary movement acquires, their place and their function within the revolution must also be debated. Revolutionary forces must fill a vital function— helping the revolution make the necessary decisions at the right moment—but effective power, in the final analysis, comes down to structures of self-organization.

This tumultuous chapter remains open. When we revisit it, we must do so with as critical an eye as possible, but without drawing a connection between the Lenin years and the Stalin years. For the rupture that occurred throughout the 1920s in revolutionary Russia did not originate in the character of individuals, but in the social forces that carried them. In the shadow of Stalin, who so ferociously descended upon the Russian Revolution, hangs the same specter that disfigured, in a different age, the French Revolution with Napoleon—the specter of counterrevolution, the eternal danger that haunts all revolutions as soon as they emerge.

The common enemy of the red and the black alike.

Revisiting the Kronstadt Tragedy

The Two Versions of the Conflict

The Kronstadt insurrection and its repression by the Soviet state in 1921 has been a bone of contention between libertaires and Marxists, and in particular between anarchists and Trotskyists, for nearly a century. Here we will try to revisit this tragic confrontation with a new perspective.

Let us briefly recall the facts. In early 1921, the Civil War in the USSR ended with the defeat of the Whites, but the country was exhausted; hunger and the rigors of war communism provoked protests. Strikes and workers' marches took place in Petrograd in February, eliciting the sympathy of the sailors of Kronstadt, a strategic fortress and the center of the Baltic fleet, situated on an island in Petrograd harbor (now Saint Petersburg, a few miles away). The military base—as well as the island and its inhabitants—had been a bastion of the revolution in 1917 and 1918. On March 1, 1921, a general assembly was convened at Anchor Square in the center of Kronstadt. Sixteen thousand sailors, soldiers, and workers gathered there. Mikhail Kalinin, the Soviet head of state, and Nikolai Kuzmin, the commissar of the Baltic fleet, were invited and received with military honors, banners, and fanfare.

The sailors of the cruiser *Petropavlovsk* prepared a resolution which was to be approved by the assembly; the votes were unanimously in its favor, save the two voices of the two representatives of the Soviet government, Kalinin and Kuzmin. The sailors' resolution demanded, among other things: the reelection of delegates to the soviets by secret ballot; freedom of speech and of the press for the workers and peasants, and for the anarchists and left-socialist parties; freedom of assembly for unions and peasant organizations; the liberation of socialist and other radical political prisoners; that the peasants be given complete control over their land, as well as the right to hold cattle, on the condition that they themselves work, without hiring employees for wages; and that free artisanal production be authorized, also without wage labor. In the course of events, some voices rose to demand the election of a Constituent Assembly, others to propose "Soviets without Bolsheviks." The motto on the front of the Kronstadt paper, the *Izvestia*, was "All Power to Soviets, and not Parties!"[1]

On March 2, a conference of three hundred delegates presided over by a sailor named Stepan Petrichenko met in Kronstadt and elected a provisional committee. Kuzmin and Vassiliev, the communist president of the Kronstadt Soviet, were placed under arrest. Radio Moscow denounced the mutiny as directed by a general of the old regime, Kozlovsky (actually present in the fortress, but not part of the movement's leadership), and inspired by French counterespionage. On March 5, the Soviet leadership (Lenin and Trotsky) delivered an ultimatum to the insurgents and declared a state of siege in Petrograd.

The American anarchists Emma Goldman and Alexander Berkman, present in Moscow and loyal to the Soviet government, sent a message (along with two others named Perkus and Petrovsky) to Grigory Zinoviev, the foremost Bolshevik leader in Petrograd, imploring him to negotiate with Kronstadt so that a peaceful solution to the conflict might be found. The text of this message is one of the most important documents of this tragic story.

Cold and hunger have produced dissatisfaction.... White-guardist bands wish and may try to exploit this dissatisfaction in their own class interests. Hiding behind the workers and the sailors, they throw out slogans of the Constituent Assembly, of free trade, and similar demands. We anarchists.... Will fight with arms against any counter-revolutionary attempt.... hand in hand with the Bolsheviki. Concerning the conflict between the Soviet Government and the workers and sailors, we hold that it must be settled, not by force of arms, but by means of comradely, fraternal revolutionary agreement.... Comrades Bolsheviki, bethink yourselves before it is too late.[2]

The American anarchists proposed sending a commission of five people to Kronstadt, including two anarchists. Zinoviev did not take up their offer. March 7 saw the first exchanges of cannon fire between Kronstadt and Petrograd.

On March 8, as the Tenth Congress of the Russian Communist Party was beginning, the Kronstadt *Izvestia* called for a "third revolution," destined to open up "a broad new road for socialist creativity."[3] Several waves of assault were launched against the island by the Red Army, and repulsed by the rebels, between March 8 and March 15. On March 15, the Tenth Congress of the Communist Party was drawing to a close, having made the initial decision to head in the direction of the New Economic Policy, allowing greater economic freedom for peasants and artisans. The following day, a general bombardment of the fortress by artillery and aircraft took place. Over the 17th and 18th, the Red Army succeeded in recapturing Kronstadt, at the cost of heavy losses on both sides. Two thousand insurgents were taken prisoner, some shot on the spot and others shot in the prisons of the Cheka over the following months (several hundred, according to Victor Serge).

For this brief recap, we used a chronology laid out in an Alternative libertaire booklet titled 1921, *L'insurrection de Cronstadt la rouge* (The insurrection of red Kronstadt), published in 2008.[4] We have made our best effort to simply sum up the facts, without passing judgment on their contents.

Two versions—or rather, two contradictory accounts, in point-by-point opposition—arise from these facts. For the Bolsheviks, with Lenin and Trotsky leading, Kronstadt was ultimately a *counterrevolutionary* movement. It was, Lenin explained in his report to the Tenth Congress on March 8, "the work of Socialist-Revolutionaries and whiteguard émigrés, and at the same time the movement was reduced to a petty-bourgeois counter-revolution and petty-bourgeois anarchism," meaning a movement of "petty-bourgeois anarchist elements, with their slogans of unrestricted trade and invariable hostility to the dictatorship of the proletariat."[5] In another of his declarations to the Congress, Lenin summed up the affair in terms that came closer to reality: "[At Kronstadt] they do not want either the whiteguards or our government—and there is no other."[6]

As for Trotsky, he repeatedly cited an article published in the French newspaper *Le Matin* in mid-February, announcing an uprising in Kronstadt, as proof that "the centers of counterrevolutionary plots are located abroad."[7] Much later, challenged by friends (or adversaries), including Victor Serge, to explain himself on this episode, he proposed a sociological explanation: the "deeply reactionary" ideas of the rebels "reflected the hostility of the backward peasantry toward the worker.... The hatred of the petty bourgeois for revolutionary discipline. The movement therefore had a counterrevolutionary character."[8] It was not until 1939, in his biography of Stalin, that Trotsky outlined a more nuanced analysis: "Suffice it to say that what the Soviet government did reluctantly at Kronstadt was a tragic necessity; naturally, the revolutionary government could not have 'presented' the fortress that protected Petrograd to the insurgent sailors only because a few dubious anarchists and SRs [Socialist-Revolutionaries] were sponsoring a handful of reactionary peasants and soldiers in rebellion. Similar considerations were involved in the case of Makhno and other potentially revolutionary elements that were perhaps well-meaning but definitely ill-acting."[9]

It is this argument above all others, that of "tragic necessity," which would be upheld by the Trotskyist movement—for example, by Pierre Frank in the introduction to Lenin and Trotsky's *Kronstadt*, which he produced and published in 1976.

The anarchist account is, of course, completely different. The theme of the "third revolution" against "the Communist yoke" had already appeared in the rebels' original declarations.[10] Writing in 1922, Alexander Berkman asserted that Kronstadt, this first step toward the third revolution, "demonstrated that the Bolshevik regime is unmitigated tyranny and reaction, and that the Communist State is itself the most potent and dangerous counter-revolution."[11] This analysis was again developed at great length in the works of Ida Mett (*The Kronstadt Commune*) and Alexandre Skirda (*Kronstadt, 1921: Prolétariat contre bolchévisme*). The latter is particularly vicious, denouncing the "Bolshevik counterrevolution" from October 1917(!). The Alternative libertaire booklet *1921, L'insurrection de Cronstadt la rouge* is more interesting. A collection of documents, it includes an introduction by Patrice Spadoni entitled "Kronstadt, ou la tragique erreur de Lénine et Trotsky" (Kronstadt, or Lenin and Trotsky's tragic mistake). Spadoni recognizes in Lenin and Trotsky "sincere revolutionaries" but thinks them responsible for "monopolization of power by a single party."[12] There is also a text that appears in the booklet, undated, signed "Libertarian Communist Movement," that tells a different story, calling Trotsky "the Gallifet of the Kronstadt Commune."[13] This text takes up the anti-Bolshevik view without much nuance: "The counterrevolution that vanquished Kronstadt was not the overt counterrevolution of the Whites, but the camouflaged counterrevolution of the Bolshevik bureaucracy."[14]

We find neither of these two one-sided accounts to be satisfying. In our view, the conflict between Kronstadt and the Bolshevik government is not a fight between "revolution and counterrevolution"—a claim common to both sides, with each reversing the roles of the protagonists—*but a tragic and fratricidal confrontation between two revolutionary currents*. The responsibility for this tragedy is shared, but falls primarily on those who held power.

A Dissenting View: Victor Serge

Victor Serge (1890–1948) was a Russo-Belgian writer and militant anarchist (he spent several years in prison in France, wrongfully accused of complicity with the Bonnot Gang) who converted to Bolshevism after 1917.[15] A friend of both Lenin and Trotsky, sent to Siberia by Stalin for his support of the Left Opposition, exiled to France and later to Mexico, he was a sort of libertarian Marxist who, despite his adherence to communism and Trotskyism, always kept an affinity for anarchist ideas. His observations on Kronstadt—which led to his falling-out with his friend Lev Davidovich [Trotsky]—are interesting, and less one-sided than the two opposed versions we have just reviewed here.

During the events of Kronstadt, Serge supported the anarchists' attempt at mediation but ultimately rallied to the Bolsheviks. It was in response to Trotsky's letter to Wendelin Thomas, published in July 1937, that he finally made up his mind on the tragic episode.

First, he refuted Trotsky's argument that "the uprising was dictated by a desire to get privileged food rations."[16] It is incorrect, he writes, that the sailors of Kronstadt demanded special privileges; they were demanding the removal of militia barricades, which were preventing the population from gathering food and supplies in the countryside.[17] On the other hand, they "formulated a demand which was, politically, extremely dangerous at that moment, but which was of general interest, disinterested and sincerely revolutionary: 'Freely elected soviets.'"[18] It would have been easy, Serge insists, to avoid the uprising by "listening to Kronstadt's grievances, by discussing them, even by giving satisfaction to the sailors," especially their economic demands, which would be addressed to a large degree by the New Economic Policy.[19]

> Even when the fighting had started, it would have been easy to avoid the worst: it was only necessary to accept the mediation offered by the anarchists (notably Emma Goldman and Alexander Berkman) who had contact with the insurgents. For reasons of prestige and through an excess of authoritarianism, the Central Committee refused this course. In all this the responsibility of Zinoviev, the President of the Petrograd Soviet, was particularly great: he had just misled the whole … city by announcing to us that "the White general Kozlovsky had seized Kronstadt by treason." It would have been easy and humane, and more politic and more Socialist, not to resort to massacre after the military victory…. The massacre that ensued was outrageous.[20]

That said, in the final analysis, Serge nevertheless chose to side with the Bolsheviks. His argument is as follows: the Kronstadt rebels "wanted to release the elements of a purifying tempest, but all they could actually have done was to open the way to a counter-revolution, supported by peasants at the outset, which would have been promptly exploited by the Whites and the foreign intervention…. Insurgent Kronstadt was not counter-revolutionary, but its victory would have led— without any shadow of a doubt—to the counter-revolution. In spite of its faults and its abuses, the Bolshevik Party is at this juncture the great organised…. force which, despite everything, deserves our confidence."[21]

Victor Serge returned to the subject a few years later in his remarkable autobiography, *Memoirs of a Revolutionary*, written in 1943. On one hand, he recognized that "Kronstadt had right on its side. Kronstadt was the beginning of a fresh, liberating revolution for popular democracy."[22] But on the other hand, "if the Bolshevik dictatorship fell, it was only a short step to chaos, and through chaos to a peasant rising, the massacre of the Communists, the return of the émigrés, and in the end, through the sheer force of events, another dictatorship, this time anti-proletarian."[23]

A point of view very close to that of Victor Serge is suggested, paradoxically, by a historian close to the libertaires: Paul Avrich, the author of extensive academic research on Kronstadt. Avrich, who refers to Serge often, sums up the perspective of his book this way: "Kronstadt presents a situation in which the historian can sympathize with the rebels and still concede that the Bolsheviks were justified in subduing them. To recognize this, indeed, is to grasp the full tragedy of Kronstadt."[24]

Serge and Avrich are right to insist on the fact that a Bolshevik defeat would have opened the path to a counterrevolution. But does this argument justify the behavior of the Soviet authorities toward the insurgents before, during, and after the fighting? In the third part of this chapter, we try to draw our own conclusion.

An Error and a Wrong

The crushing of the sailors of Kronstadt was not "a tragic necessity," but an error and a wrong. It is not a question of rewriting history, nor of looking to discharge ourselves of a part of our heritage that is impossible to bear—even though there would be no shame in that. It is a question, rather, of drawing the appropriate conclusions from this event in order to envision the future.

The murderous suppression of the Kronstadt revolt was a brutal decision that goes back to an inexcusable error. The

Kronstadt Soviet was not a nest of counterrevolutionaries. That counterrevolutionaries tried to infiltrate, manipulate, or profit from its struggle is probable. However, not everything has to do with conspiracies. Moreover, the nature, history, functioning, and vitality, as well as the demands of this soviet clearly attest that Kronstadt was well within the camp of the Revolution of 1917, not that of the Old Regime. This does not mean the sailors of Kronstadt are exempt from all critical examination. Some of their demands are debatable, and may sometimes seem fanciful in view of the economic and political emergency in a country ruined by years of civil war against the Whites and a good part of the world. But for all that, nothing in the resolution they adopted is reprehensible as such. The words about the Communist Party and the proposals made may seem crude, but there is a deeper question at play—namely, that of the grip of the Bolshevik Party on revolutionary society. The motion demanded the end of the party monopolization, not the end of soviet power. Quite the opposite—it rebuked the Party for ossifying the power of the soviets. If there is a problem, then, it must be found elsewhere.

It is true that, beyond its contents, the motion is charged with an act of defiance toward the central government—an act well worth assessing. Did the sailors really understand all the unintended consequences of dividing the revolutionary camp at that particular moment? To have done so would have objectively run the risk of opening up a breach, to the benefit of the counterrevolution—which would entail them feeling themselves suited to hold such a possibility in check. It is a question, here, of appreciating the political moment.

Whatever the case may be, however debatable the act may be, it remains without comparison to the heavy responsibility of the Bolsheviks in this fratricidal drama. Through Zinoviev, they refused the proposal for mediation from the internationalist anarchists like Emma Goldman. From that point on, the break was irreversible. Trotsky was not to be outdone:

although he did not personally participate in the bloody repression, he all the same took time to leave the session of the tenth congress in Moscow to go on the radio and deliver, in his capacity as commissar for war, the ultimatum addressed to the population of Kronstadt. Above all else, he also accepted, supported, and defended the crackdown. Still more appalling and deplorable (for us, two authors who come out of a traditionally Trotskyist organization), much later, in 1937—his struggle against the Stalinist bureaucracy then in full swing—when he revisited the Kronstadt conflict, Trotsky showed no remorse for this disaster, save calling it a "tragic necessity," "reluctantly" undertaken.[25]

In fact, despite his pertinent analysis and theoretical reflection on bureaucratization, Trotsky did not know or want—indeed, could not—understand or admit that these events fueled this process. They are the sign of a devitalization of revolutionary power, not its reinforcement. The choice of the Bolshevik Party consisted of imagining, a priori, the military option as the sole response to the demands of the Kronstadt Soviet. Yet Kronstadt had participated in the Russian Revolution from the beginning, whatever changes in social composition it may have undergone.[26] In plain language, the crushing of Kronstadt signified that, in the soviets, there was no longer any place for freely debating the course of the revolution. Beyond the complex and terrible circumstances of the civil war, which offered few possibilities, the crackdown, with its political and military violence, caused even more of a short circuit for the self-management option in Russia. What good would it do to give more power to the soviets if the idea that they served only to obey the orders of the party had begun to enter into the popular imagination?

Trotsky himself left behind some antibureaucratic tools that betray the fact that the Stalinist counterrevolution was already at work at the time of the Kronstadt uprising. Stalin's takeover of the party would come only a year later, during the eleventh congress in April 1922. It was not an event that took place overnight. During the Kronstadt insurrection, the apparatchiks in the Kremlin did not yet have a total hold on the party, they had not yet robbed the soviets of the revolution, but they were gradually moving in that direction. In this context, the crushing of the marines at Kronstadt was a service—and not a disservice—to their ascension to power, a power that from then on could not be contested. Does that not necessarily mean that we must also see in the Kronstadt revolt proof that, potentially, there still existed forces at the beginning of the revolution that were open to fighting against the growing bureaucratization? It is easy to ask this question now, a century later.

However that may be, the adage that the end justifies the means is already questionable in itself; it is even more so when set in the context of a conflict that pits revolutionaries against each other. This wound between red and black is far from healed. Yet the work of reaffirming our points of solidarity also entails revisiting this episode of the Russian Revolution.

Makhno: Red and Black in Ukraine (1918–21)

In the book of disputes between libertaires and Marxists, Nestor Ivanovich Mikhnienko, or "Makhno" (1889–1934) occupies a prominent place. For the same reasons as the sailors of Kronstadt, his name evokes the discord between the two revolutionary families. Here too, temporary alliances were made and then, tragically, broken.

In his work *Makhno: la révolte anarchiste*, Yves Ternon chronicles the episodes of this unconventional revolutionary's epic life.[27] Born to a poor peasant family, Makhno's entire life took place in double time. He began working early, at the age of ten. At seventeen, he became an active member of the anarcho-communist group of the region, in Huliaipole. His participation in the group's radical actions—a policy of "black terror" (setting fire to large landholdings, assassination attempts on the local governor)—led him straight to the central prison of Moscow in 1908 for nine years of imprisonment. There he met the anarchist activist Peter Arshinov, with whom he completed his radical education. The doors of his prison were opened a month after the February Revolution of 1917. Upon his return to Ukraine, he found his old comrades and formed the Peasants' Union, which, spurred on by the revolutionary turmoil, became a veritable local soviet. The Peasants' Union led the collectivization of land and the expropriation of factories. Makhno actively participated in its communal committee.

The Brest-Litovsk peace treaty, signed in March 1918, changed the game: it planned the dismantling of the Russian Empire and reserved a peculiar fate for Ukraine—the return of German rule, and in its wake, the return of the large landowning families. Social and national questions became intertwined. At harvest time, a few months into 1918, the peasants found themselves suddenly dispossessed of their harvest by military requisitioning; thus, they realized the cruelty of the foreign military occupation. Makhno traveled to Moscow to find support and prepare a counterattack. There he met the anarchist Peter Kropotkin, with no significant results. Lenin gave him "a friendly reception" at his office in the Kremlin, according to Victor Serge.[28] In his memoirs, Makhno himself relates their civil and sincere discussion. Concerning Lenin, Makhno mentions his "deep regard" for "a man with whom there would have been a lot more topics to explore and from whom there would have been a lot to learn."[29] During their encounter, still according to Makhno, Lenin was at no loss for words himself, even if his compliment was ambiguous: "You, comrade, I regard as a man with a feeling for the realities and requirements of our times. If only a third of the anarchists in Russia were like you, we Communists would be ready to work with them under certain conditions and work in concert in the interests of free organization of the producers."[30]

Makhno returned from his stay in Moscow convinced that the time was ripe for organizing a peasant guerrilla force. So he took action. Victor Serge, who was no idealizer of Makhno's character ("boozing, swashbuckling, disorderly, and idealistic, [Makhno] proved himself to be a born strategist"),[31] outlines the source of the momentum that would carry him to the head of the rebellion for more than three years: "Among the peasants of the Ukraine, their spirit of rebellion, their capacity for self-organization, their love for local autonomy, the necessity of relying on nobody but themselves as defense…. gave rise to an extraordinarily vital and powerful movement…. The anarchist Nabat (or Alarm) Federation provided this movement both with an ideology, that of the Third (libertarian) Revolution."[32] The "Makhnovtsi" had been born.

Led by a red and black cavalry unit whose standard bore the slogan "Land and Freedom," the peasant army began its long journey. From its origins in September 1918, this peasant insurrection would go on to liberate Ukraine, combining military exploits and the will to organize a new society, relying on anarchist precepts—the army functioned on the principles of voluntary participation and elections, and the land was self-managed by the peasants and the collectivized villages.

This revolutionary episode is a new example of the chaotic history of pacts and splits with the Red Army. The two armies wasted no time in forming an alliance against the czarist White Army led by General Denikin. But Makhno refused the slightest Bolshevik supervision. Although early relations with the government had been established fraternally, the anarchist did not share the centralist notions of the Soviet authorities and was wary of their potential duplicity. On this point, the facts prove him right. And so, the agreement established in January 1919 with a Ukrainian Soviet commander, Dybenko, was never really respected.[33] With Trotsky's arrival at the head of the Red Army in late May 1919, there was no end in sight to the rupture between Makhno and the Bolshevik government, which tried its best to quell a movement that it deemed rebellious and uncontrollable—they issued an order banning local meetings, and an order of arrest and execution for the general staff of the Makhnovtsi.

Strong off their victory over Denikin's troops in late September, the Makhnovtsi, however, enjoyed growing prestige among the population—these were the peasant army's political and military glory days. But the different peasants' and workers' congresses in Ukraine failed to equip themselves with their own democratic structure, and never joined forces with the urban working class, which, for that matter, they never really pursued. Here the momentum of the revolution ran up against the old tenets of anarchism, poorly suited to such a level of overarching political organization. Furthermore, the world of military matters is not necessarily the most favorable to libertaire principles, and Makhno, an unparalleled organizer, showed himself to be a leader—the *batko* (or little father) of Ukraine—with a tendency toward authoritarianism.

Victor Serge, opposed to the suppression of the Revolutionary Insurrectionary Army of Ukraine, took the liberty of emphasizing that as far as democratic virtue is concerned, everything is not necessarily black or white—red or black—and that every movement knows its share of contradictions in the face of the reality of events: "I have no doubt that they [Alexander Berkman and Emma Goldman] were just as disconcerted and indignant over a good deal of what happened in Makhno's movement."[34] The fact remains that the strength of the Makhnovtsi consisted in conducting their own experiment, driving back the Whites and defying the Bolshevik authorities by their autonomous functioning. In so doing, they wrote one of the most original pages in the history of the libertaire movement.

Their success was frustrating to some. The arrival of the Red Army in the south of Ukraine at the end of December 1919 raised the tension a notch, and marked the beginning of the open conflict that would, from that point on, set red and black against each other. In January 1920, troubled by the growth of the Makhnovtsi, the Bolsheviks proclaimed the movement "outlaws." A ruthless struggle unfolded over several months, leaving tens of thousands dead. The short peace that arose after the two parties signed a new treaty in October 1920—to work together against Denikin's successor, Baron Wrangel—ended as soon as victory over the Whites was achieved in November. The fratricidal combat began again with renewed violence. The Bolsheviks mobilized their troops and hunted Makhno down.

Assailed and pursued by the Red Army over several long months, he fled, wounded, to Romania in August 1921, in the company of a few dozen followers. Upon his arrival, with his family, in France in 1924, he did not give up the struggle, but took up more theoretical activities instead. In 1926 he got involved with the Group of Russian Anarchists Abroad and created *the Organisational Platform of the General Union of Anarchists,* which fought to equip libertaire revolutionaries with a direction and a system of organization. In doing so, he distinguished himself from supporters of the "synthesis" perspective, such as Voline and Malatesta; he thought their organizing principles were impractical, and that they transformed political organizations into conglomerates of different currents, heterogenous and powerless. He also distanced himself from anarcho-syndicalism, which he saw as too focused on urban workers and limiting itself to making the trade-unionist movement more anarchist. As for those subscribing to anarchist humanism,[35] a current focusing on cultural development rather than political or economic action, he found them to be too far removed from the struggle against capital. Building on the impasse of individualist anarchism, "platformism" aspires to act as a complement to anarcho-syndicalism and thereby "gather its forces into one organization, constantly agitating, as demanded by the reality and strategy of the social class struggle."[36] In 1927, he received two Spanish libertaires, Buenaventura Durruti and Francesco Ascaso of the National Confederation of Labor, and convinced them of the necessity of his organizing principles. They would later put them into practice during the revolution in Catalonia, in 1936. Two years before the promising barricades went up in Barcelona, Makhno died in France, in July 1934.

III

A Few Libertarian Marxist Thinkers

Walter Benjamin (1894–1940)

Walter Benjamin occupies a unique place in the history of modern Marxist thought, for his ability to incorporate elements of the Romantic critique of civilization, the Jewish messianic tradition, and anarchist thought into the theory of historical materialism. Indeed, he sought to articulate, combine, and fuse anarchist and Marxist communist ideas. This initiative is one of the most remarkable characteristics of his thought.

It was in early 1914, during a lecture on student life, that Benjamin first made reference to a revolutionary libertaire utopia. He contrasted utopian images, both revolutionary and messianic, with the formless and meaningless ideology of linear progress, which, "trusting in the infinity of time, distinguishes only the tempo, rapid or slow, with which human beings and epochs advance along the path of progress."[1] He paid homage to the liberal arts and sciences, "alien and often hostile to the state," and aligned himself with the ideas of Tolstoy and "the most profound anarchists."[2]

In his 1921 essay "Critique of Violence," we find reflections that are directly inspired by Georges Sorel and anarcho-syndicalism. Benjamin does not hide his total disdain for state institutions, like the police ("the greatest conceivable degeneration of violence") or parliaments ("woeful spectacle").[3] He approves without reservation the antiparliamentary criticism of the Bolsheviks and the anarcho-syndicalists as "annihilating and on the whole apt"—explicitly identifying the two currents as being on the same side—as well as the Sorelian idea of a general strike that "sets itself—the sole task of destroying the state power."[4] This outlook, which he designates as "anarchist," is commendable to him because it is "deep, moral, and genuinely revolutionary."[5]

In a document from the same period (which remained unpublished during his lifetime), "The Right to Use Force" Benjamin explicitly describes his own thinking as anarchist: "An exposition of this standpoint is one of the tasks of my moral philosophy, and in that connection the term 'anarchism' may very well be used to describe a theory that denies a moral right not to force as such but to every human institution, community or individuality that.... claims a monopoly over it."[6]

It is therefore evident, from these early documents of 1914 21, that Benjamin's first ethico-political choice was anarchism—the radical and categorical rejection of all established institutions and, in particular, of the state. It was only later—strangely enough, after the end of the great European revolutionary upsurge of 1917–23—that he discovered Marxism. The events in Russia and Germany undoubtedly made him more receptive to Marxist ideas, but it was only in 1924, by reading Georg Lukács's *History and Class Consciousness*, and meeting the Latvian Bolshevik teacher and activist Asja Lācis (with whom he fell in love) during a vacation in Italy, that he really become drawn to Marxism, a way of thinking that would soon become a key component of his political and theoretical reflections.

The first of Benjamin's works in which the influence of Marxism is visible is *One-Way Street*, an odd collection of notes, commentaries, and fragments about the Weimar Republic, during the years of hyperinflation and the crisis of the interwar period. Written from 1923 to 1925, it was published in 1928. It is interesting to note that in this work the only revolutionary political current mentioned is anarcho-syndicalism.

In a fragment curiously entitled "Minister of the Interior," Benjamin examines two ideal types of political behavior: (a) the politically conservative man, who does not hesitate to put his private life at odds with the maxims that he defends in public life, and (b) the anarcho-syndicalist, who ruthlessly subjects his private life to the norms upon which he wants to base the laws of a future social state.[7]

The most important of Benjamin's Marxist-libertaire documents is without a doubt his 1929 essay "Surrealism: The Last Snapshot of the European Intelligentsia." From the first paragraphs, Benjamin describes himself as "the German observer," situated in a "highly exposed position between an anarchistic *fronde* and a revolutionary discipline."[8] Nothing conveyed the convergence so ardently desired between these two poles in a more concrete or active way than in 1927, when in the streets of Paris, communists and anarchists marched together in demonstration and riot against the conviction of the US anarchists Sacco and Vanzetti. The surrealists were present, and Benjamin celebrates the "excellent passage" from André Breton's 1928 book *Nadja*, where he refers to "the delightful days spent looting Paris under the sign of Sacco and Vanzetti." "Breton adds the assurance that in those days Boulevard Bonne-Nouvelle [Good News] fulfilled the strategic promise of revolt that had always been implicit in its name," Benjamin writes.[9]

It is true that Benjamin had a very broad understanding of anarchism. Describing surrealism's distant origins (and future path) he writes, "Between 1865 and 1875 a number of great anarchists, without knowing of one another, worked on their infernal machines. And the astonishing thing is that independently of one another they set its clock at exactly the same hour, and forty years later in Western Europe the writings of Dostoyevsky, Rimbaud, and Lautréamont exploded at the same time."[10]

The date, forty years after 1875, is of course a reference to the birth of surrealism, particularly with the 1924 publication of the first *Manifesto of Surrealism*. Though Benjamin designates the three authors—Dostoyevsky, Rimbaud, and Lautréamont—as "great anarchists," it is not simply because Lautréamont's "erratic book" belongs to the insurrectionary tradition, or because Rimbaud was a Communard.[11] It is above all because their writings, whether novels or poems, blew up—like Ravachol's dynamite or the Russian nihilists, in another context—the bourgeois moral order, the "moralizing dilettantism" of the *Spiesser*[12] and the Philistines.[13]

The libertaire dimension of surrealism shows itself just as directly, Benjamin says, in that "Since Bakunin, Europe has lacked a radical concept of freedom. The Surrealists have one."[14] In the immense body of material written about surrealism over the course of the last seventy years, it is rare to find a phrase as vivid, as capable of expressing, in a few simple, biting words, the core of the movement founded by André Breton. According to Benjamin, it was "the hostility of the bourgeoisie toward every manifestation of radical intellectual freedom" that pushed surrealism toward the left, toward revolution, and—after the Rif War[15]—toward communism.[16] In 1927, of course, Breton and his surrealist followers joined the French Communist Party.

This tendency toward politicization and growing commitment did not, in Benjamin's view, mean that surrealism had to abandon its magical and libertaire qualities. On the contrary, Benjamin believed those qualities allowed it to play a unique and irreplaceable role in the revolutionary movement: "To win the energies of intoxication for the revolution—this is the project about which Surrealism circles in all its books and enterprises. This it may call its most particular task."[17] In order to accomplish this task, however, surrealism must be willing to abandon a unilateral stance and accept an alliance with communism: "It is not enough that, as we know, an ecstatic component lives in every revolutionary act. This component is identical with the anarchic. But to place the accent exclusively on it would be to subordinate the methodical and disciplinary preparation for revolution entirely to a praxis oscillating between fitness exercises and celebration in advance."[18]

There are almost no explicit references to anarchism in Benjamin's last writings. However, for an acute observer such as Rolf Tiedemann—the editor of the first German edition of his complete works—his last texts "can be read as a palimpsest: under the explicit Marxism the old nihilism becomes visible, which risks leading to the abstraction of Anarchist practice."[19] The word "palimpsest" is perhaps not the most appropriate: the relation between both components, for Benjamin, is not a mechanical one of superposition, but rather an alchemical combination of substances previously distilled by the author, in his own way.

It was in early 1940 that Benjamin wrote his "political testament," the essay "On the Concept of History" (also known in English as "Theses on the Philosophy of History"), one of the most important documents in revolutionary thought since Marx's *Theses on Feuerbach*. A few months later, he attempted to escape from Vichy France and its police, who were tracking down antifascist German exiles and Jews in general. Arriving at Cerbère, on the French coast, he crossed the Pyrenees with a group of refugees and made it across the border, but on the Spanish side Franco's police arrested them and threatened to hand them over to the Gestapo. And so, in the Spanish village of Portbou, Walter Benjamin chose suicide.

Rolf Tiedemann, in his analysis of "On the Concept of History," remarks that "Benjamin's idea of political praxis.... Has more of the enthusiasm of the anarchists than the sobriety of Marxism."[20] The problem with this statement is that it opposes as mutually exclusive precisely the two ideas, the two approaches that Benjamin tried to associate, because they seemed to him complementary and equally necessary for revolutionary action: libertaire "enthusiasm" and Marxist "soberness."

André Breton (1896–1966)

Author of the 1924 *Manifesto of Surrealism*, André Breton can be considered the "inventor" (in the alchemical sense) of surrealism. Driven by the desire to break with bourgeois Western civilization, Breton took interest in the ideas of the October Revolution, as shown by his 1925 review of Leon Trotsky's *Lenin*. Though he joined the Communist Party of France in 1927, he still reserved, as he explained in the pamphlet *Au Grand Jour* (In broad daylight),[1] his "right to criticism."

The 1930 *Second Manifesto of Surrealism* drew the logical conclusions of this act. In it, Breton affirms "completely, without any reservations, our allegiance to the principle of historical materialism."[2] While emphasizing the distinction—the opposition, even—between the "primitive materialism" and "modern materialism" (as Friedrich Engels would have said), he insists that "Surrealism considers itself ineluctably linked, because of certain affinities I have indicated, to the movement of Marxist thought and to that movement alone."[3]

It goes without saying that his Marxism did not coincide with the official vulgate of the Soviet Comintern. It belongs, in any case, like that of José Carlos Mariátegui, Walter Benjamin, Ernst Bloch, or Herbert Marcuse (all drawn to surrealism!) to what might be called a Romantic Marxism—that is to say, a Marxism fascinated by certain cultural forms of the precapitalist past, but which transforms this nostalgia into a force in the struggle for the revolutionary transformation of the present. It is through André Breton's surrealism that the Romantic revolutionary attempt to *reenchant the world* reaches its most striking expression.

This adherence to communism and Marxism did not change the fact that there existed, at the very heart of André Breton's approach, an irreducibly libertaire position. It is enough to recall the profession of faith of the first *Manifesto of Surrealism*: "The mere word 'freedom' is the only one that still excites me."[4] This libertaire dimension undoubtedly contributed to the fact that Breton and most of the surrealists (except Louis Aragon) chose to break definitively with Stalinism in 1935. This was in no way a rupture with Marxism, which continued to inspire their analyses, but with the opportunism of Stalin and his acolytes, who "unfortunately tend[ed] to annihilate the two essential components of the revolutionary spirit,"[5] namely, the spontaneous refusal of the living conditions offered to human beings and the vital need to change them.

In 1938, Breton visited Trotsky in Mexico. Together, the two men wrote one of the most important documents of the revolutionary culture of the twentieth century: the "Manifesto for an Independent Revolutionary Art," which contains the famous passage: "To develop intellectual creation an anarchist regime of individual liberty should from the first be established. No authority, no dictation, not the least trace of orders from above! ... Marxists can march here together with anarchists."[6] As we know, this passage was penned by Trotsky himself, but one might also imagine it as the product of his long conversations with Breton on the shore of Lake Pátzcuaro.

Breton's anarchist sympathies manifested more clearly in the postwar years. In *Arcane 17* (1947) he recalls the emotion he felt when, as a child, he discovered a tombstone in a cemetery bearing the simple inscription "Ni Dieu Ni Maître" (No Gods No Masters). Commenting on these words, he raises a general reflection: "Above art and poetry, whether we wish it or no,

ANDRÉ BRETON

flies a flag alternately red and black"—two colors between which he refused to choose.

From October 1951 to January 1953, the surrealists contributed regularly to the newspaper Le Libertaire, the organ of the French Fédération anarchiste, publishing articles and columns. Their principal correspondent at the Fédération at that time was the libertarian communist Georges Fontenis. It was in the context of this connection that Breton wrote the flamboyant work "The Tower of Light" (1952), in which he recalls surrealism's anarchist origins: "It was in the black mirror of anarchism that surrealism first recognized itself, well before defining itself, when it was still only a free association among individuals rejecting the social and moral constraints of their day, spontaneously and in their entirety."[7] True to this origin, Breton expresses his sympathy for the anarchist movement, "[which] our comrade [Georges] Fontenis describes 'as socialism itself, that is, the modern demand for dignity of humans (their freedom as well as their well-being).'"[8] In 1953, Breton broke with Fontenis's Le Libertaire, but he did not cut ties with the libertaires, continuing to collaborate on some of their initiatives.[9]

This interest in—and active sympathy for—libertarian socialism, however, did not lead him to renounce his support for the October Revolution or the ideas of Leon Trotsky. In a speech on November 19, 1957, he was adamant: "Come what may, I am one of those who still find, in the memory of the October Revolution, a great deal of that unconditional momentum that carried me toward it when I was young, and which implied total self-sacrifice."[10] With a nod to an old 1917 photograph of Trotsky in his Red Army uniform, he proclaimed, of Trotsky's gaze: "such a gaze, and the light that rises in it, nothing can ever extinguish that, no more than Thermidor could have altered the features of Saint-Just."[11] Finally, in 1962, in a tribute to Natalia Sedova [Trotsky's wife], who had just died, he yearned for the day when, at last, "not only would justice be rendered to

115

Trotsky, but the ideas for which he gave his life would be called again, to take on their fullest strength and their fullest scope."[12]

In conclusion, surrealism and André Breton's thought are perhaps the ideal vanishing point, the supreme place of the mind where the anarchist and revolutionary Marxist trajectories meet. But we must not forget that surrealism contains what Ernst Bloch called "a utopian excess," an excess of black light that surpasses the limits of all social or political movements, however revolutionary they may be. This light emanates from the unbreakable dark core of the surrealist spirit, from its obstinate quest for the gold of time, from its headlong dive into the abyss of dreams and wonders.

Daniel Guérin (1904–1988)

The relationships between Marxists and anarchists are contentious, but they are also historically and ideologically interlinked. They have overlapped from the very start, when the labor movement took its first steps in the First International, or during the first revolutionary syndicalist wave. In the twentieth century, the missed opportunity for red and black to come together in the Russian Revolution drove the two families apart. Paradoxically, for some militants, this split has given birth to a kind of quest for an as-yet-unfulfilled reunion. Daniel Guérin was one of them. A writer (he was the author of over twenty works), historian of emancipatory movements, and unwavering militant of the anticolonial struggle and the LGBTQ cause, he was also one of the most foremost anarchist thinkers in France to be receptive to the synthesis between Marxism and anarchism. His life explains this double allegiance: he followed, in a sense, the ideological path taken by Victor Serge some years before, but in the opposite direction—he passed from Marxism to anarchism. Like him, Guérin switched camps completely and never sought to return to his first love, or to live on the political frontier between the two families. He became a full-fledged anarchist. But in the same way as Victor Serge, he wished to keep the best of his past commitment, and imagined the possibility of a mutual enrichment.

Guérin began his activism in the 1930s, as both a revo-lutionary syndicalist alongside Pierre Monatte, and as a revolutionary socialist alongside Marceau Pivert; in this partisan framework, he participated in the struggles of the revolutionary Left within the French Section of the Workers' International. "As I entered, on this momentum, into the revo-lutionary movement.... I was, right from the start, viscerally anti-Stalinist,"[1] he recounts in the foreword of his book À la recherche d'un communisme libertaire (In search of a libertar-ian communism). Through his activism and from his readings, he said he gained an understanding that "caused the scales to fall from [his] eyes, unveiled the mysteries of capitalist surplus value, taught [him] historical materialism."[2] Reading Bakunin in the 1950s had the effect "of a second cataract surgery," making him "forever allergic to all versions of authoritarian socialism, whether it called itself Jacobin, Marxist, Leninist, Trotskyist."[3] This synopsis must not overshadow the fact that behind this great bifurcation in Guérin's thought and practice, there is an activist who seeks himself, questions himself, tries several political paths and samples from many causes. A tireless anti-colonial militant, from Indochina to Algeria, he maintained a period of correspondence with Trotsky, was an active member of the Parti socialiste unifié, and participated in the founding of the Mouvement communiste libertaire in 1971.

He took something away from each of these phases and never fully severed the theoretical cord linking his many engagements. He saw changes in course as complementary and was suspicious of any definitive breaks: a red and black strand connects each of these periods.

Thus, after having distanced himself from Marxism, he never forgot to maintain some theoretical bridges with it, and by the same token, envision the synthesis of a libertarian Marxism. In 1966, in his tellingly entitled book, Frères jumeaux, frères ennemis (Twin brothers, enemy brothers), Guérin was already preoccupied with salvaging the best of each tradition, starting from the assumption that "anarchism is inseparable from Marxism," and that "to oppose them is to create a false problem."[4] Going against the trend—imposed by the history of the first half of the twentieth century—of distancing the two, he reaffirms the necessity of a shared perspective between "two variants, closely related, of a single socialism and communism, one and the same."[5] Beyond "family squabbles,"[6] the common origins are indelible—there is some anarchism in Marx and in Lenin; some Marxism can be found in Bakunin. Of course, considerable differences of opinion exist between those who support the immediate abolition of the state after the revolution and those who imagine holding onto another state, destined for its own extinction, during a transition period.

Guérin imagined that political convergences would come about through the productive confrontation of ideas. It is a matter, essentially, of "divergent means" of arriving at a "long-term strategy [that] is, all-in-all, identical": "To overthrow capitalism, abolish the state, do away with all guardians, entrust the social wealth to the workers themselves."[7] He wrote that Marx's 1871 address, written after the fall of the Paris Commune, had to be seen as "a point of departure in the effort today to find a synthesis between anarchism and Marxism, and as a first demonstration that it is possible to find a fertile conciliation of the two streams of thought."[8] Guérin was profoundly convinced that "socialism, somewhat discredited, could once again be invigorated if we succeeded in injecting a good dose of anarchist serum into the Marxisms of today."[9] This "anarchist serum" is workers' self-management, federalism, revolutionary syndicalism, as well as the centrality of the individual in a collective emancipatory project.

Daniel Guérin fought for this objective throughout his life, and never gave up presenting libertarian communism as an alternative to both "degenerate authoritarian Marxism" and "old, outdated, and fossilized anarchism."[10] His constancy and his determination to maintain ties are infectious, and his appeal is an urgently topical one: "By taking a bath in anarchism, today's Marxism can emerge regenerated and cleansed of its blemishes."[11] That bath is more necessary now than ever.

IV

Policy Issues

Individual and Collective

We must acknowledge that on the historical scale, the anarchist movement has held the flag of individual emancipation much higher than the Marxist family. The totalitarian, necrotic dictatorship of Stalinism, carried out in the name of communism, has much to do with this. In instituting a crude version of collectivism, "barracks communism" denied the individual, limiting him to his obligations to the apparatchiks and the state, under the guise of serving the community first. But for all that, this tragedy cannot erase everything, and if we take a closer look, red-black cooperation exists in matters of the place of the individual as well. In both camps, those who understand refuse to oppose the individual to the collective, the *I* to the *we*, the particular to the global or the singular to the universal. For on the other side of the mirror, there is a corresponding anarchist version just as outrageous, just as deformed as the perverted collectivist project of "barracks communism," found in certain currents of anarchism that reject not only all forms of organization or collective life, but loathe even the idea of a community with a shared fate. In this, they claim to draw their inspiration from one of the forerunners of individualist anarchist thought, the German philosopher Max Stirner (1806–1856).

In his work *The Ego and Its Own*, Stirner delivers a plea for the "ownness" of the individual, which incites each person to not abandon the self, and to free himself from all forms of alienation; he claims for each individual an inalienable right to personal liberty against all forms of oppression, be they moral or institutional.[1] Running counter to the widespread anti-individualism of early nineteenth-century philosophical currents, he foresaw the threat that the specter of the state could potentially hang over the project of individual rights in Germany. This ownness, according to him, takes on a form necessarily in contradiction with all collectivist or communist perspectives. What's more, it is opposed, still according to his theory, even to the idea of "common life" or of a "people." Shared liberation becomes incompatible with individual liberty. He rejects the notion of collective "consciousness." It's a curious take on the self-sufficient individual, for is building oneself personally on renouncing the other not already, in part, renouncing oneself?

Even as he claims Stirner as one of his own, the libertarian communist Daniel Guérin suggests that there is a complementary relationship between the individual and the collective, drawing on the philosophical reflections of Michael Bakunin (1814–1876): "Bakunin attempts to create a bridge between individuals and mass movements." To quote him: "All social life is simply this continual mutual dependence of individuals and the masses. Even the strongest and most intelligent individuals.... Are at every moment of their lives both promoters and products of the desires and actions of the masses." Guérin concludes: "The anarchist sees the revolutionary movement as the product of this interaction."[2]

Even though it may defy our preconceived notions, there exists, paradoxically, in Marx's thought—particularly in the works he produced as a young man—a joyful individualism that the perversion of excessive collectivism has not destroyed. In his *Economic and Philosophic Manuscripts of 1844*, Marx reaffirms the degree to which the individual is not a means, but very much an end in itself. The ultimate objective of communism is the individual fulfilment of each person. Capitalism, in transforming all sequences of human activity into commodities, divides up the individual, "fragments" it. "Each of his human relations to the world—seeing, hearing, smelling, tasting, feeling, thinking, observing, experiencing, wanting, acting, loving—in short, all the organs of his individual being" have been alienated by the law of profit.[3] Later, in 1867, in *Capital*, he explores this idea in greater detail, contrasting the *being* of the "complete" man with the *having* of the man "fragmented" by capitalist alienation.[4] The latter is estranged by the division of labor, he is dispossessed of his production by the law of value: by their labor, wage-earning workers transform raw materials into commodities and therefore give them a surplus value, of which only a very small portion comes back to the producers in the form of wages. The individual, caught in the pincers of the double nature of labor and in the circuits of capital, is systematically separated from a part of himself, from his social time, from his production, from his work—from an activity that is his to begin with. Capitalism is not individualistic; it oppresses the individual.

The contribution of Marxism to the conception of the individual—to his defense against capital—is not insignificant. It is Marx's writings, for example, that form the political basis of the revolutionary humanism of Ernesto "Che" Guevara. Che found in the *Manuscripts of 1844* the Marx who "analyzed the problem of man's liberation and saw communism as the solution to the contradictions that brought about his alienation"; he found in *Capital* the Marx who cultivated a "humanistic character (in the best sense of the word)."[5] He prefers a communism that he refers to as "the society of communist human beings," where collective and individual share a complementary and balanced relationship, to the "individual cage" that encloses our personalities.[6] The people are not an anonymous and obedient mass, but "a multifaceted being [which] is not, as is claimed, the sum of elements of the same type (reduced, moreover, to that same type by the ruling system), which acts like a flock of sheep."[7]

If it is therefore essential to "re-individualize" the communist project, it is just as necessary to "collectivize" anarchist ideas. The balance between the particular and the global is delicate; finding it is fundamental. To denigrate the individual is surely to follow in the footsteps of totalitarianism, but renouncing all notion of the collective inevitably ends in retreating into oneself. The universal can be found in the particular just as much as personal identity can unfold in one's relation to others. Far from egoist, agoraphobic individualism or Playmobil socialism, a revolutionary humanist path remains open. Che Guevara liked to quote the Cuban poet and revolutionary José Marti often: "Every true man must feel on his own cheek every blow dealt against the cheek of another."[8] From this profession of faith his genuine internationalism was born: one cannot feel authentically free, as an individual, while others are enslaved.

A radical new approach to contemporary individualism is necessary, as the critical sociologists Philippe Corcuff, Jacques Ion, and François de Singly call for, among other things, in their work *Politiques de L'individualisme*.[9] Even the notion of individualism used to be considered, paradoxically, as an aberration—the negation of the individual. In the nineteenth century, the revolutionary Auguste Blanqui (1805–1881) spoke already of "that individualism which, for thousands of years, has continuously killed both freedom and the individual."[10] He added, "Communism safeguards the individual; individualism [that of capital and of the moralists] exterminates it. For the one, every individual is sacred. The other cares for individuals as much as it does for earthworms."[11] A century and a half later, capitalist globalization is a system that has given birth to new personal needs, beyond solely consumerist aspirations, in terms of access to culture, knowledge, travel.... But the reign of capital, being what it is, cannot satisfy these aspirations for more than a small minority even as it creates them in the greatest possible number. Reintegrating the individual dimension and not abandoning this terrain to the liberals calls us to a twofold task. First, it entails integrating this dimension into the vision of society that we defend for tomorrow, which must— especially, and now more than ever—include the questions of racist, sexist, and sexual oppressions, and of personal liberties. On this point alone freedom of expression takes, with the advent of the Internet, a new turn in the relationship that it establishes between the individual and the group: this is one of the lessons of the use of social media, for example, in the Arab Spring, or the Indigné or Occupy movements. But granting a central role to a sharing individualism also implies changing our militant practices, *here and now*. Which forces us to ask: What type of political representation do we want to build?

Today it is important that we break with the established patterns of politics that divide the world in two—those who know and those who don't—and begin instead with the assumption that each of us knows and is capable of something. The French philosopher Jacques Rancière, for example, in his numerous works—and especially in his book *The Ignorant Schoolmaster*[12] or the collection of his interviews *Dissenting Words*[13]—invites us to depart from a point of everyone's intellectual equality, rather than our presupposed intellectual inequalities, and to accept this feature of individualism as a concern for legitimate emancipation, which frightens the ruling classes: "This is how the dominant intellectual discourse meets up with those censitaire[14] and knowing elites of the nineteenth century: individuality is a good thing for the elites; it becomes a disaster for civilization if everybody has access to it."[15] Politics, even radical politics, if understood only as a matter of the hierarchical division of knowledge, perpetuates the break between the people, the individual, and political organizations. Professional politicians, who fear the interference of the masses in political life, have an interest in this—but radicals do not. This chasm, this caesura, is at the heart of the Indigné and Occupy movements that so recently shook the world. These movements proclaim "*We* are real democracy, now" and at the same time demand of each person a strictly individual participation in it.

At the heart of the new period that opened with the fall of the Berlin Wall in 1989, a multitude of more or less successful initiatives have shown the will to make possible "the expression of the self," to borrow the language François de Singly uses in "Pour un socialisme individualiste" (For an individualistic socialism).[16] This pursuit touches on aspects of the personal and the collective—one of the reasons that dignity found (again) is one of the themes that routinely appears in these struggles. To become indignant today begins with a highly individual act, a gesture of resistance that may appear insignificant but which nevertheless requires mobilizing the internal strength that waits within each of us, (finally) speaking up. That, if nothing else. The first refusal that pushes each of us to force ourselves to go against our inhibitions and to give ourselves new meaning, is already, in part, a removal of the chains of the contemporary alienation that exploits us as much as it encourages us to remain silent, stifled as we are by the gag of our own acceptance. Is it not the goal of activism, to begin with, to offer this liberty? Is the undertaking not first of all a source of personal enrichment? From this point of view, it seems that there is an urgent need to install new "software" in the life and functioning of our twenty-first century revolutionary organizations, be they Marxist or libertaires.

Making Revolution
without Taking Power?

For a good part of the Left, even the revolutionary Left, social change takes place mainly through the state, or state power, which it is a question of "taking." This leads to a concept of "revolution from above," which in turn leads, sooner or later, to the distortions of authoritarianism and bureaucracy.

Inspired by the Zapatista movement of Chiapas, John Holloway, an Irish political intellectual living in Mexico, published in 2002 a book entitled *Change the World without Taking Power: The Meaning of Revolution Today*, which had considerable impact in anarchist, autonomous, and antiauthoritarian circles, particularly in Latin America.[1] It is an influential book, driven by an authentic anticapitalist rage; whatever its limits and its weaknesses may be, it is an impressive display of the critical and subversive force of negativity. Its objective is ambitious and timely: to render more acute the Marxist critique of capitalism.

Holloway's criticism of statist concepts of "taking power," whether by social democracy or by Stalinism, is as pertinent as his calling into question the notion of vanguardist guerrilla forces who intend to "take power" in the name of the people. Our principal disagreement concerns Holloway's thesis itself, which gives the book its title: changing the world without taking power. It rests primarily on three theoretical arguments.

The first is the observation that the currently existing state is a part of capitalist social relations. However, as Holloway himself recognizes, revolutionary Marxism is aware of this overlap—its objective is not to seize the existent state, but to smash it and create another in its place. The second argument is that the state as such, whatever its social content may be, is a fetishized form.[2] This comes from the classic anarchist argument, shared to a certain degree by Marx, most notably in his writings on the Paris Commune, in which he saw the impulse toward a non-statist form of political power. This form, which he designates a "Communal Constitution," can only emerge by "the destruction of the State power," that "parasitic excrescence" that he saw "feeding upon, and clogging the free movement of, society."[3] The third argument—the most important, and the one that runs throughout the book—is new. It concerns the distinction between *power-to*, the ability to get things done, and *power-over*, the power to command others to do what you want. Revolutions, according to Holloway, must promote the former and suppress the latter. We are not convinced by this distinction: in our opinion, there can be no form of collective life or social action among human beings without some form of power-over.

These objections to Holloway's central thesis have to do with the idea of *democracy*, a concept that is practically absent from the book, or at least is treated in passing in a rather scornful way, as a sort of election-influenced state control over the decision-making process. We think, on the contrary, that democracy should be a central feature of all social or political decision-making processes, and especially revolutionary ones—a thesis outstandingly argued by Rosa Luxemburg in her (fraternal) critique of the Bolsheviks in 1918.[4] Democracy means that the majority has power over the minority. Not absolute power—it has its limits, and it must respect the dignity of the other. But all the same, it has a *power-over*. This applies to all sorts of human communities, including the Zapatista villages Holloway refers to.

For example, in 1994, after a few weeks of combat, the Zapatistas decided to stop shooting and negotiate a truce. The Zapatista villages debated this decision, and a majority—or perhaps there was a consensus—declared that the armed struggle should cease. The minority—if there was one—had to either accept this decision or necessarily break with the Zapatista movement. The majority had power over the minority. The villages then gave the order to the commanders of the Zapatista Army of National Liberation (EZLN) to cease fire— they had power over their military leaders. And finally, the commanders themselves, obeying the orders from the villagers, instructed the combatants to cease fire—they had power over them. We do not claim that this is an exact description of what happened, but it is an example intended to show that democracy brings forms of *power-over* into play.

The principal objection we have to the concept of power developed by Holloway is its extremely *abstract* character. He mentions the importance of bringing memory to resistance, but there is very little memory, very little history, in his arguments, as he hardly discusses the merits or limits of real, historical, revolutionary movements, be they Marxist, anarchist, or Zapatista. In one of the rare passages where he mentions a few positive historical examples of self-determination, he refers to "The Paris Commune discussed by Marx, the workers' councils theorized by Pannekoek, the village councils of the Zapatistas."[5] Yet it can easily be shown in each of these cases there were forms of democratic power that exerted a certain form of *power-over*. We have already discussed the practices of the municipal councils of the Zapatistas.[6] What, then, of their proposals for Mexico?

Holloway's book is, to some extent, a brilliant commentary on the Zapatistas' principles of revolutionary action: "We do not want to take power!" Yet this declaration must be associated with another EZLN slogan: "For everyone, everything. For us, nothing." If we put these two affirmations in contact with the fight for democracy in Mexico, which has a prominent place in the Zapatistas' proclamations, we find the following argument: "We, the Zapatista Army of National Liberation, do not want to take power ourselves, we want power for the people, meaning a real democracy."

The Paris Commune produced a new form of power that was no longer a state, in the conventional sense, but which was nonetheless a government, democratically elected by the people of Paris—in a combination of direct and representative democracy—and it had power over the population by its decrees and its decisions. The Commune had power over the National Guard, and the commanders of the National Guard had power over their soldiers. And this power, the democratic power of the Paris Commune, had been literally "taken," first of all by the act of taking possession of the material instruments of power—the cannons of the National Guard.

Finally, as far as the council communist Anton Pannekoek—a severe critic of Lenin—is concerned, he wanted "all power to the workers' councils," and he conceived of the councils as a means for the workers to "seize power and to establish their mastery over society."[7]

What is also missing from Holloway's discussion is the concept of *revolutionary praxis*, first formulated by Marx in his *Theses on Feuerbach*. This concept, it seems to us, is the real answer to what he calls "the tragedy of fetishism" and its dilemmas: how can people so deeply enmeshed in fetishism liberate themselves from the system? Marx's answer is that through their own emancipatory praxis, people change society and change their own consciousness at the same time. It is only by their practical experience of struggle that people can liberate themselves of fetishism and take power. This is also why the only true emancipation is self-emancipation and not liberation from above. Any self-emancipatory action, individual or collective, however modest, may be a first step toward revolutionary transformation.

Autonomy and Federalism

Power at the Human Scale

Communism, to begin with, intends to entrust as many powers as possible to the base and foster local initiatives. This is the very essence of the democratic project that it includes: the idea that we should be able to decide about the things that concern our daily lives, because they concern *our daily lives*. We are the ones who are primarily concerned, yet the system, in removing the decisions made about our daily lives from our field of vision, robs us of our fate, placing it instead in the hands of professional politicians and merchants. Not only are we the most affected by these choices, but objectively, we are also the most qualified to carry them out. The ability to do so is not a matter of credentials or prerogatives; quite the opposite. Whether in municipalities or corporations, *we* remain in the best position to know what to do, for whom and with whom. Within their neighborhoods, the residents are the best suited to evaluate the resources that should be allocated for housing, schools, public transit, and social life. In the offices, the workshops, and the service industries, the workers know better than anyone how to organize the sensible production of goods and the coherent delivery of services. Better, in any case, than many of the bosses deciding or organizing them. We must not fall into demagoguery here: certain tasks of coordination require specific activities that cannot be carried out by the endless deliberations of assemblies. Deciding everything in common all the time is impractical. But the regular and effective involvement of each and every person can be promoted, for example, by allowing for assembly-style meetings during working hours. Furthermore, the tasks of coordination need not be individualized to the extreme; they can be subjected to rotation as well as the vote, without acting in practice as favoritism for any one individual. Whatever the case may be, a de-hierarchization of politics (in the spirit of the old adage, "hierarchies are like shelves: the higher they go, the less useful they are") can be carried out in the businesses as in the municipalities by means of workers' self-management. This would submit the collective choices to the democratic control and deliberation of everyone, instead of continuing to leave them to the bosses and other powerful people to decide without our knowledge. Bringing politics back to the human scale, locally, daily, is the only way to give power to the base, to share it between everyone by placing it within anyone's reach. The only way to collectivize it, by ourselves.

At the beginning of the twentieth century, many revolutionaries, especially anarchists, idealized this or that particular form of local power: some imagined the new society as a federation of communes, others as a federation of trade union halls. In reality, decisions must be made in local assemblies in the workplace as in the places of residence. Both are necessary, because direct, authentically participative democracy is indispensable for assessing the needs of civil society just as much as it is for organizing production after the fact, according to the demands duly expressed by the population. It is the only way to be done with the capitalist schizophrenia that splits us into two opposing categories—wage earners / consumers— and thereby rediscover the sensible, unified individuality of the producer-citizen. Communism, socialism, libertaire self-management, whatever name we may give it, fundamentally comes down to one notion: the community of "freely associated producers" evoked by Karl Marx.

Federalism and Conscious Coordination

Generalized autonomy is one thing, but it doesn't mean that everything can be decided locally. International relations, major manufacturing decisions, industrial policy, public services, public transit, heavy infrastructure, energy options, the fight against climate change, the exhaustion of our natural resources.... Many subjects will not withstand self-management. It is a question of allowing everyone, no matter where they may be, to provide for their well-being and not allow, in the name of autonomy or the necessity of short-range economic or agricultural circulation, the separation of wealthy regions from those of scarcity to continue. Moreover, the self-management of production and of municipalities must be appropriately aligned. And finally, the local management of industry by the workers themselves does not mean, for example, maintaining economic competition between units of production as the market demands. The financing of industry must be secured by a unified public credit authority that distributes the funds to those that need them according to the demands determined by the collective choices of democratic economic planning. Self-management entails permanent changes in scale, through a close relationship between the local and the global. There is no a priori contradiction between encouraging, on one end, maximal autonomy in the democratic organization, and on the other, building a common destiny with all peoples. The centralization and coordination of all these activities is unavoidable, from local regions to entire continents. The issue is guaranteeing that this cooperation is controlled by the base. This means that only those decisions that cannot be objectively made at the local level should be delegated to a higher level. Within businesses, unification can be carried out by regular assemblies at the level of professional branches, and then at the interprofessional level when it comes to the production of goods or services. Within society, territorial units can likewise coordinate their actions through regular assemblies. To determine major policy guidelines or implement global production according to local requests, a permanent assembly that brings together delegates from municipalities and industries will be needed to debate and resolve everything that cannot be decided locally. In the event of disputes, consultations can be arranged by the base councils; popular referendums can also be called in the event of disagreements. Delegates should be recallable by the bodies that elect them. A percentage of the electoral body can also be empowered to call a new vote if they feel that their mandate is not being respected. These assemblies, debates, and deliberations should have it as their objective to advance the process past potential sticking points, and hence get the delegates to change their positions as needed. Ultimately, the delegates should remain as close as possible to the original mandate delivered by the base and can be removed if their position changes in a way that is not shared by the electing assembly.

In order to stimulate the creative capacity of this process, democratic discussion is vital. On the way forward through this transition, people must be able to express all points of view freely, and to group themselves into parties.

From the idea of federalism developed by the anarchists, we can retain the focus on power to the base and voluntary solidarity between collectives. The Marxists, for their part, have insisted that this coordination will inevitably become corrupted if civil society allows it to be carried out "spontaneously," according to the capitalist rules of supply and demand. What, then, is the fundamental difference between the idea of "consciously planned coordination" (as opposed to the "spontaneous coordination" of the market) articulated by the Marxist Ernest Mandel and the "self-managing democracy" envisioned by Daniel Guérin?[1] Each, in its own manner, attempts to suggest paths to building a large, free, and interdependent association. There is no template or prefabricated, easy-assembly kit to provide us with all the answers, only the will to see a real democracy emerge, actually working from the bottom up, liberated as much from administrative despotism and bureaucracy as from the dictatorship of capital.

Democratic Economic Planning and Self-Management

Self-management is a proposal common to libertaires and non-Stalinist Marxists. Ernest Mandel, the principal theorist of the Fourth International, in the preface to his 1973 anthology *Contrôle ouvrier, conseils ouvriers, autogestion* (Workers' control, workers' councils, self-management), emphasizes "the *universal* character of the workers' tendency to seize their businesses and reorganize the economy and society on the basis of principles that correspond to their self-determination needs."[1]

Revolutionary Marxists have the greatest admiration for the extraordinary experiment in agrarian and industrial collectivization fostered by the National Confederation of Labor–Iberian Anarchist Federation during the Spanish Revolution of 1936–37, which brought the self-management of farms and factories into a regional—and national—federative organization. Since then, Marxists and libertaires have found themselves together, side by side, supporting every attempt by the workers to take back their factories and make them run in their own name. Such was the experience of the French watchmaking company LIP in the 1970s, and, albeit on a larger scale, that of the workers in Argentina after the financial crisis of 2001, as shown in the Naomi Klein film *The Take*.[2] Marxists and libertaires also share a rejection of the watered-down version of self-management, a reformist self-management compatible with capitalism, such as the one championed, in France, by Michel Rocard's so-called Deuxième Gauche (Second Left) and the French Democratic Confederation of Labor from the late 1970s into the 1980s.[3]

In a pamphlet recently published by the Fédération anarchiste, two Latin American libertaires put forward a definition of self-management that we find interesting: "For anarchism, self-management is a project whose method and objective are that industry and the economy be directed by those who are directly connected to the production, distribution, and use of goods and services."[4] Thus, the two authors recognize that self-management is not limited to each factory or school, that it extends to all of society, but that we cannot do without some forms of delegation "for limited periods, revocable at any time."[5] This understanding is not so different from that of Ernest Mandel: "Self-administration does not entail the disappearance of delegation. It combines decision-making by the citizens with stricter control of delegates by their respective electorate."[6]

Where are the disagreements? The anarchists, in the name of self-management, reject the Marxist concept of *economic planning*, generally associated with the disastrous Soviet experiment. But what is democratic economic planning, if not self-management extended to the whole of society? The failure of the USSR illustrates the absurdities of flagrantly inefficient and arbitrary bureaucratic economic planning, but it cannot be used as an argument against truly democratic economic planning. The socialist conception of economic planning is nothing more than the radical democratization of the economy—if it is true that political decisions should not fall to a small group of ruling elites, why not apply the same principle to decisions of an economic order? The whole of society would be free to democratically choose which lines of production to encourage and the level of resources to be invested in education, health, or culture. The prices of goods themselves would no longer answer to the laws of supply and demand but would be determined as much as possible according to social, political, and ecological criteria.

Democratic socialist economic planning is not inconsistent with workers' self-management in their production units. While the decision to transform, for example, an auto factory into a production unit for buses or trolleys, would come down to the whole of society, the organization and internal functioning of the factories would be democratically run by the workers themselves. The "centralized" or "decentralized" character of economic planning has long been debated, but the important thing remains democratic control of the plan at all levels: local, regional, national, continental—and, let us hope, global, for the current ecological trends, such as climate change, are global and can only be dealt with at the same level. This proposal, which could be called "democratically self-managed society," or "global democratic economic planning," does not correspond in the least to what is often described as "central economic planning," for the economic and social decisions are not made by any sort of "center," but determined democratically by the populations concerned.

There would be, of course, tensions and contradictions between the self-managed establishments or local democratic administrations and other, broader social groups. The mechanisms of negotiation can help to resolve many conflicts of this sort, but in the final analysis, it would be up to the largest groups concerned to exercise their democratic right to decide. To give an example: the decision to shut down a nuclear power plant cannot be made solely by the workers at that establishment. This is a question that concerns the whole of society. On the other hand, the dismantling of the plant—an operation of several years, if not decades—would be organized in a self-managed way, by the workers themselves. Questions like access to free public transit, the subsidizing of solar energy, and the banning of pesticides and GMOs concern the whole of society and not only a limited group of "direct producers."

One conception of self-management that has become popular in many libertaire milieus is the "participatory economy," or "Parecon" as conceived by Michael Albert. This proposal, which recognizes the need for some sort of economic planning, has some characteristics in common with the democratic socialist economic planning that we are proposing here: opposition to the capitalist market and to bureaucratic economic planning, confidence in workers' self-organization, and antiauthoritarianism. Albert's model of participatory economic planning is founded on a complex institutional construction:

> Workers and consumers negotiate outcomes based on full knowledge of effects. They have proportionate influence in decisions. The facilitation board announces what we call "indicative prices" for all goods, resources, categories of labor, and capital stocks. These indicative prices are calculated based on the prior year's experience and knowledge of general changes since. Consumers, consumer councils, and federations respond with consumption proposals, taking the indicative prices as estimates of a true valuation of all the resources, equipment, labor, bad byproducts, and social benefits associated with each good or service."[7]

At the same time, individual workers, their councils and federations, also make their own offers for production, with all the inherent calculations of cost and price, a way of estimating the social value of production.

> Receiving the public proposals from workers, consumers, and their councils, the facilitation boards calculate the excess demand or supply for each good and mechanically adjust the indicative price for the good up or down in light of the new data and in accord with socially agreed formulas for these alterations.... Since

no participant in the planning procedure enjoys an advantage in influence over any other, and since each participant impacts the valuation of social costs and benefits like all others do, but with each having more impact on what they are involved in producing and consumers and less on what they aren't affected by, the procedure generates equity, efficiency, and self-management simultaneously.[8]

The main problem with this conception is that it seems to reduce "economic planning" to a sort of negotiation between producers and consumers about the prices, resources, finished products, supply, and demand. There is no place, in this model, for an issue of socialist ecology. A postcapitalist ecological perspective entails the total elimination of certain sectors of industry—for example, nuclear power plants—and massive investment in sectors that are practically nonexistent (like solar energy); how can all that be managed by "cooperative negotiations" between the existing production units about "resources" and "indicative prices"?

Albert's model returns to currently existing structures of technology and production, and is too "economist" to take into account the sociopolitical and socio-ecological interests of the population—the interests of individuals as human beings and citizens, living in a threatened natural environment, who cannot be reduced solely to their economic interests as producers and consumers. In his conception, it is not only the state as an institution that is cast aside—which is a respectable choice—but also *politics* as the confrontation of different choices, be they of an economic, social, political, ecological, cultural, or civilizational order, at the local, national, and international level. Without this (radically democratic) political dimension, self-management would be impossible.

Direct and Representative Democracy

The opposition between representative democracy and direct democracy is one of the subjects that has divided anarchists and Marxists since the nineteenth century. Without underestimating these very real disagreements, some significant convergences can still be found. For example, both are favorable to forms of direct democracy in social struggles: general assemblies, self-organized strikes and pickets, etc. Marxists also recognize that many of the criticisms of representative democracy, from Rousseau to Cornelius Castoriadis, Proudhon, and Bakunin, and entirely justified:

The citizen is not free except for the day on which they elect their representative. In the four or five years that follow, they are without power; the professional politicians form a privileged class, a political oligarchy (Bakunin) in service of the ruling classes and not the people who elect them; parliaments are strangers to the interests of the population, and their debates—the parliamentary circus—remove all control or participation from the dominated classes.

We might add that the electoral mechanisms are corrupted by money, by the media (in the hands of the moneyed interests), by the historical exclusion of women, the current exclusion of immigrants, etc.

Revolutionary Marxists are in agreement with the anarchists that it is not through these institutions that we will be able to transform society. Should they, under these conditions, participate in the electoral spectacle, present candidates, vote and be elected? For Marxists, yes, insofar as electoral campaigns—with their obvious limits—are a rare occasion for them to present their analyses and proposals to the wider population. For another thing, those elected—local council members, representatives—can use parliaments or local councils as a platform to denounce the system and propose radical alternatives. And finally, in some cases, it becomes necessary to vote for the reformist-left candidate, when it is the only way to block the path of the reactionary Right. Of course, none of these practices is acceptable to those anarchists who refuse all forms of participation in state institutions. This principled abstention could be considered unrealistic; elsewhere, under certain conditions—exceptional ones, it is true—anarchists, despite their politics, have decided to participate in elections, such as in Spain in 1936, when they voted for the Popular Front.

This question of electoral participation is perhaps a pragmatic one, but it plays an important role in the practices of these two currents, and contributes to their separation in everyday political action. Our point of view in this debate is closer to the Marxist tradition, but we recognize that even the most radical Marxist organizations are not immune to the dangers of electioneering and parliamentarism denounced by the anarchists.

To come back to the abovementioned criticisms, does the anarchist critique concern the "actually existing" forms of representative democracy, meaning the parliamentary institutions of the bourgeoisie, or rather the *principle itself* of political representation? The distinction isn't always very clear in the writings of the classical anarchist thinkers (Proudhon, Bakunin, Kropotkin). For example, according to Bakunin: "The system of democratic representation is a system of hypocrisy and perpetual lies."[1]

In fact, the revolutionary experiments claimed by both Marxists and anarchists—the Paris Commune, the workers' councils of 1917–19, the Spanish Revolution of 1936—all *combined* forms of direct and representative democracy. The Commune of 1871 was an assembly of delegates elected (and recallable) by the universal suffrage of the districts of Paris; the soviets were councils of delegates elected in the assemblies (of the factories, soldiers, villages, etc.); in the insurgent Barcelona of 1936, the revolutionary power was, during the early period, in the hands of committees of delegates elected by the antifascist militias of the National Confederation of Labor–Iberian Anarchist Federation. In the Zapatista movement of Chiapas, one of the primary sources of inspiration for libertaires in the twenty-first century, we also find forms of delegation: the election of commanders—and sub-commanders!—in the Zapatista Army of National Liberation and in the local authorities of Zapatista communities, often local assemblies.

In our opinion, the same reasoning applies to the prospects of an emancipated society, beyond capitalism and its state. What would its political institutions be? There exists a tendency, as prevalent within the Marxist tradition as within the anarchist one, to think that a free society has no need for politics. The nineteenth-century French philosopher Henri de Saint-Simon spoke of "replacing the government of persons by the administration of things," (a statement later taken up by Engels), and Proudhon claimed that politics would give way to the economy. We do not share this economicist idea. We believe that socialist (or communist) societies will always need politics, in the noble sense of the collective management of the city and the democratic organization of communal life. Differences of opinion, even conflicts are inevitable—nothing would be more dismal than a society in total and unanimous agreement where there exists but one sole opinion! This is, in any case, impossible, at least without the imposition of a totalitarian power. We must therefore find ways to permit debate and democratic decision-making.

Without presupposing the forms that this politics of the future will take, it seems to us that it cannot be limited to the direct democracy of assemblies. Though valid at the level of the factory, school, or neighborhood, it is unworkable at the level of a large city, region, country, or—even less so—continent. Certain forms of delegation, of political representation, are inevitable. Libertaires seem to recognize this in proposing measures that limit the corruption of representation: the revocation of mandates, popular referendums, the drawing of elected officials by lottery, etc.: these proposals strike us as interesting, as do the experiments—with all their limits—in participatory democracy (such as at Porto Alegre). The only general rule that we might propose is the necessary combination of direct and representative democracy, neither of the two, in isolation, being able to meet the needs of effective popular participation. The revolutions of the future will undoubtedly invent new forms of politics, perfectly unpredictable, which will not repeat the experiences of the past.

Union and Party

On the social and political Left, unions and parties share the quality of being collective groupings of individuals that intend to speak for the workers. They are the two primary faces of the labor movement. This common definition accords the party an electoral perspective, with the intention of influencing governmental policy, and the union the strict framework of the defense of the interests of wage laborers. The institutionalization of politics and unions over the past century has unfortunately made this definition a rather good summary of the actual situation: a strict dividing line. Thankfully, things remain more open than this. The union-party relationship, it is true, does not look the same in every country. And so, in the United Kingdom, in Brazil, or in Kanaky, for example, the organizations are historically and organically linked, and this generates no debate.[1] In France, on the other hand, the connection is tangled and convoluted. This complex relationship does not mean there are no interesting experiments—the reinvigoration of social movement in France in 1995, marked by huge social mobilizations, caused a new type of syndicalism and class struggle to appear, one independent of political parties, yet still affirming of radical political choices. This was particularly the case with the Sud-Solidaires unions.[2]

Unions are a vital reflex of the working class and necessary places of resistance, as long as they are combative, radical, and unified. They are, moreover, spaces where societal choices are legitimately debated, beyond the multiple political sensibilities that exist within them. The political parties that declare themselves for radical political change seek to give the daily struggles a constancy, a consciousness and a memory that resist the fluctuations of society and politics. This political outlet, which comes from the movement itself, proposes to give it an overall vision and a direction so that the mobilization actually amounts to something. In other words, so that the revolutions are not continually dispossessed by the regimes in place, and so that they can arm themselves with a strategy capable of allowing the exploited to take the power out of the hands of their exploiters. Unfortunately, the real history of the labor movement is, from this point of view, a long series of missed connections. The revolutions of the nineteenth century, perhaps, suffered from the absence of a revolutionary party at the decisive moments of confrontation between the classes— this was especially the case with the Commune in 1871. Those of the twentieth century unfortunately often suffered from their omnipresence, with parties that, as they became more bureaucratic, substituted themselves for the revolution—as in the Russian Revolution of 1917, for example.

Whatever we might think of it, the paradox remains intact: though revolutions can do without organizations to get themselves started, on the other hand they need an independent organizational perspective to reach their ends. A synthesis of the social and the political, then, must be defined.

From World War I onward, bureaucracy started to take over the union world. The time of unions as "transmission belts for the parties" arrived, as well as that of "apolitical" unions that above all else did not get involved in antigovernment activities. These are, in fact, the two sides of the bureaucratic coin. This syndicalism bears heavy responsibility for the labor defeats of the past.

To imagine syndicalism, then, as an alternative in itself to bureaucratic drift has always been an illusion, whether for the laborers' France of 1900, or the revolutionary Russia of 1920. Alexandra Kollontai and the Workers' Opposition within the Bolshevik Party in 1921, during the Tenth Congress of the Russian Communist Party, believed that trade unionism would be a bulwark against the bureaucratization of Soviet society. Perhaps it came as a response to the instrumentalist notion of militarizing the unions, as championed by Trotsky. But it was a mirage all the same, as the evolution of the Confederation of Labor in France had already shown. What's more, to think of trade unionism as the embryonic federation that could organize production tomorrow poses an additional difficulty: history teaches us how a totalitarian state can manipulate unions and stifle democratic life in the world of labor on the pretext of giving the union the legal power to manage industry. Furthermore, pluralism has established itself as a reality that cannot be ignored. What is true in this realm for the union is also true for the party.

The time of the rhetoric of "class *is* the party," promoted by Stalinism, is quite fortunately behind us. Let us remember Rosa Luxemburg's beautiful words in *The Russian Revolution*, written in 1918: "Freedom is always and exclusively freedom for the one who thinks differently."[3]

In short, the fetishization of forms of organization, whatever they may be, is always a danger. No organization, political or union, can claim to hold a monopoly on the movement. Yet this fetishism often takes root in issues concerning the means of action. Thus, in the early twentieth century, the truncated debate about the general strike that so strongly divided the labor movement proved to what point two apparently diametrically opposed understandings could produce the same result, unfortunately for the worst. Indeed, the parliamentary socialists, who supported gradual change, were strongly opposed to the strike becoming widespread, deeming it too impetuous and much less attractive than the intoxicating charms that the state offered them from then on. As for the CGT, on the pro-union side, despite its rhetoric about the general strike, it would also, under the leadership of Léon Jouhaux, join the Sacred Union in the summer of 1914, as did many socialists.

The general strike therefore also calls for a mediation between the social and the political. In the debate within the German Social Democratic Party, in the early twentieth century, Rosa Luxemburg proposed an answer, one opposed to Kautsky and the reformist leadership of the party. She drew her lessons from the first Russian Revolution of 1905 and its spontaneous experimentation with soviets. Although strongly affected by the context of German political life, where the "united" party-union relationship was built at the expense of the union, Rosa's conception of the "political mass strike," expressed in her book *The Mass Strike, the Political Party and the Trade Unions*, deserves a moment's consideration.[4] According to her, the general strike cannot be decreed. It is the fruit of the spontaneous emancipation of the masses rising up against injustice. Furthermore, she envisions this movement as a collective experience of political self-education, where the central question of change, that is to say, of taking power, is posed on a mass scale. The debate shifts: the general strike is neither fetish nor foil. It then becomes a matter of being open and favorable to it, of preparing oneself for it, in order to enrich the mass movement with a political direction that, at the decisive moment of the social confrontation, will allow it to vanquish the counterrevolutionary forces.

There is no set organizational solution to the project of liberation. Each historical episode delivers its share of lessons. For example, enticed by the momentum of the Russian Revolution of 1917, the proletariat in several countries, each in turn, committed to the experiment of workers' councils. First in Germany in 1918, then in the north of Italy in 1919, and again in Hungary in 1920. In Italy, the mobilization of the workers of Turin in 1919 and 1920, for example, allowed millions of workers to control their production. As a first step, union strikes sought to give "internal commissions" the power to make decisions in the factory. The lockout by the bosses that followed left the workers de facto to fend for themselves. Over the course of this experiment in self-management, the Italian anarchists and Marxists stuck close together, including through the organization of the journal *Ordine Nuevo* in which, among others, the revolutionary socialist Antonio Gramsci participated. This collaboration lasted until the creation of the Italian Communist Party in 1921.

The experience of councils is an indisputable form of self-organization which reappears frequently in the history of workers' struggles and which, without being a template exportable to every context and era, is just as valid today as it has ever been. In contrast, "council communism" theorizes the functioning in councils as a means and an end in itself. This concept was notably developed by the Dutch revolutionary Anton Pannekoek (1873–1960) in his 1947 book *Workers' Councils*.[5] His thought falls within a perspective of self-liberation and within the antiauthoritarian socialist tradition. He deserves credit for opting for the socialization of the means of production under the control of the producers themselves, rather than for their nationalization from above. But for all that, in excluding the role of parties and unions, his political thought, in its consistency, slips toward sectarian shortcomings: the councils cut themselves off from the immediate action of the masses by ignoring intermediary political mediations. These, however, are necessary to establish a power relationship favorable to the wage-earning class and to make them aware of their own strength. This conquest of self-confidence is the prelude to self-organization. Thus, this theory does not escape the impasse of those who seek, at all costs, to find a stable, successful, and permanent organizational solution to the emancipation of the masses.

Every period delivers its share of experiments with their successes and failures. Through them, the past offers a compass for action: self-organization. Self-organization is the structuring of the mobilization by the masses themselves. It involves organizing the struggles in a unified way, within the framework of regular and sovereign general assemblies, open to all workers who want to mobilize. Organizations can participate in these assemblies, but without looking to substitute themselves for the natural organ of the struggle. The assemblies can, within their ranks, elect a committee of delegates, dismissible, to ensure the carrying out of everyday tasks. They can also, when the movement grows beyond the local framework, elect delegates, also dismissible, to participate in a coordination where the delegates from different assemblies meet to unify their activities. The self-organization of struggles is of interest for two reasons: It sets up a legitimate, unitary, and common framework between different organizations, which often allows for protection against the poison of division that leaders often distill. What's more, the power to make decisions belongs to the base, which arms the mobilization against attempts at bureaucratic takeover. This democratic option for organization prefigures today the way society could function tomorrow. It is also the best point of entry for giving constructive meaning to the party-union relationship.

Miracle solutions do not exist, and behind the fetishization of organizations (unions, parties, etc.) or of forms of struggle (general strikes, occupations, the "cretinism of legality" or the "romanticism of illegality," to borrow the words of the Hungarian Marxist Georg Lukács) many political shortcuts arise.[6] Complexity is in order. The conflicting relationships of multiple organizational forms, beyond ideological fractures, amount to the necessary dialectical relationship between the social movement and the political alternative. Radical syndicalism and a revolutionary political force, both adapted to the new issues of the twenty-first century—this is what we must build, in a complementary relationship.

Ecosocialism and Anarchist Ecology

Marxist and anarchist militants have found themselves together, shoulder to shoulder, in very real ecological struggles: against nuclear energy, against GMOs, against fracking, and in the movement for climate justice. Nevertheless, both revolutionary currents were slow to integrate ecology as an essential component of their platforms; the resistance to going beyond the ideology of progress, and "worker-ist" productivism/industrialism was considerable.

All the more reason to recognize the pioneering role of the American anarchist thinker Murray Bookchin, who laid the foundations of a libertarian socialist ecology in the 1960s. In an essay published in 1964, "Ecology and Revolutionary Thought," he advanced several fundamental ideas, ahead of their time, with which we can only agree. A declared opponent of capitalism, Bookchin observed that the competitive nature of bourgeois society set not only each human being against the others but also the whole of humanity against the natural world. The result is the destruction of the environment on a global scale; more concretely, the massive use of fossil fuels produces the accumulation of carbon dioxide in the atmosphere, with serious disruptions of the climate, likely leading to the melting of the polar icecaps and the submersion of vast stretches of land. In other words: fifty-five years ago, when very few people were worried about these questions, Bookchin was sounding the alarm, with striking precision, about the dangers of global warming.[1]

A few years later, in an essay titled "Toward an Ecological Society" (1974), he went on the offensive again: the degradation of the environment has infinitely deeper causes than the errors or bad intentions of manufacturers or the state; the environmental crisis plunges its roots into the structure of present society itself. The real alternative, then, can only be "a fundamental, indeed revolutionary, reconstitution of society." "One might more easily persuade a green plant to desist from photosynthesis than to ask the bourgeois economy to desist from capital accumulation," he adds with biting sarcasm.[2] Despite his opposition to Marx's political concepts, Bookchin recognizes the relevance of his critique of the political economy: "Accumulation is determined not by the good or bad intentions of the individual bourgeois, but by the commodity relationship itself, by what Marx so aptly called the cellular unit of the bourgeois economy. It is not the perversity of the bourgeois that creates production for the sake of production, but the very market nexus over which he presides and to which he succumbs."[3]

The dynamic of accumulation inevitably leads to the collapse of the biosphere and the disappearance of the organic conditions of human life. We must therefore create an ecological society, in a break with capitalism, "not merely because such a society is desirable but because it is direly necessary."[4] Every word of this analysis is accurate, and even more current today than it was forty-five years ago.

Where to begin? We have no illusions, he observes, as to the possibility of even partially realizing such a way of life within a society of death. We must not passively wait for the ecological millennium, but hold our ground, block the construction of nuclear plants, highways, large, useless projects[5] — all while keeping present in our minds this rigorous alternative between ecotopia and ecological disaster. In imagining this ecological utopia, we have much to learn from supposedly "primitive" societies: those organic communities, still present among Indigenous peoples around the world, that maintain a sense of symbiosis, interdependence, and cooperation with nature.

Up to this point, we can only admire Murray Bookchin's coherence and clear-sightedness. Where, then, are the disagreements? First of all, with his surprising technological optimism: Bookchin seems to believe that modern technology—automated machines and computers—will carry us from "the realm of necessity" to "the realm of freedom,"[6] creating the possibility of "material abundance for all, even.... The disappearance of toil as an underlying feature of the human condition."[7] He goes so far as to cite "the Ford plant in Cleveland," where, thanks to automation, three hundred workers were replaced by "a few monitors to watch the automatic control panels."[8] What seems untenable to us in this approach is not only the lack of critical distance toward existing technologies, but also, and above all, the illusion of "abundance," of a "post-scarcity" economy—as if the planet's resources were not limited![9]

Like many libertaires, Bookchin insists on economic and political decentralization, direct democracy, the abolition of bureaucratic and political hierarchies, the management of social life by popular assemblies of local communities—what he sometimes calls "libertarian municipalism."[10] He often cites the ancient Greek *polis* as a model where collective decisions were made by the assembly of citizens, after a face-to-face meeting and discussion—in our opinion, a somewhat idealized vision of the Athenian *ecclesia*, which excluded slaves, foreigners, and women, meaning the overwhelming majority of the population! Bookchin sometimes seems to reject not so much capitalism as "corporate gigantism with its immense, incomprehensible industrial installations," which must be replaced by "small units [of production]," quoting, not without naivety, E.F. Schumacher: "small is beautiful."[11] And above all, he carries the cult of localism so far as to propose making local communities of entities that are "politically independent" and economically autarkic (self-sufficient): "the management of society" must remain in the hands of the popular assembly of the local community.[12]

Yet, as much as we share concerns for decentralization, the relocalization of production and consumption, and the power of local assemblies (or those defined by type of activity, such as factories, hospitals, etc.), it seems impossible to us to overlook the democratic management of broader levels of economic life— regional, national, continental, intercontinental. The autarky of small units of life is not only regressive, but impossible on a planet of several billion inhabitants. Murray Bookchin seems, reluctantly, to recognize this, writing, "I do not claim that all of man's economic activities can be completely decentralized."[13] He himself cites the fact that "behind a single yard of high-quality electric wiring lies a copper mine, the machinery needed to operate it, a plant for producing insulating material, a copper smelting and shaping complex, a transportation system for distributing the wiring—and behind each of these complexes other mines, plants, machine shops and so forth."[14] But then, how to organize the production process between all these businesses? Bookchin leaves us dissatisfied. For if these businesses are autarkic, it is only by the *market* that they can exchange their products. One small problem: the market, the commercial relationship, is, as Bookchin explicitly says, quoting Marx, "the cellular unit of the bourgeois economy."[15]

Ecosocialism, which shares many of Bookchin's ideas, sees in ecological and democratic economic planning the only real alternative to the mercantile logic of capital, an alternative that is not contradictory, as we have seen, to the local self-management of factories, neighborhoods, and cities. Murray Bookchin refers to socialist economic planning with a critical mind in a 1965 essay "Toward a Liberatory Technology." His argument is as follows: the Marxist notion of a planned economy is the expression of a socialism that, in Marx's time, still carried the defect of a relative rarity of goods—hence this need to plan and rationalize the production and distribution of goods.[16] To which we respond simply: (1) the limits of the planet prevent us from entertaining the illusion of a world "without scarcity"; (2) if the production and distribution of goods are not democratically planned, that means that they are left to the market; (3) and a radical ecological reorganization of production, with the abolition of entire branches of industry and of fossil fuels, the intensive development of new sources of energy, the replacement of car and road transportation by train and urban public transit, etc.—all of this cannot be taken on at the level of small, autarkic communities. Without democratic economic planning, there can be no eco-social revolution.

CONCLUSION

Toward a Libertarian Marxism

What is *libertarian Marxism*? To try to give it a (definitive?) definition would be a mistake. That has not been the objective of this modest work. By revisiting the history, and providing a little food for thought on controversial questions, we thought it useful to begin construction, to prolong a movement, to outline the theoretical and practical convergences so that a new space might open up. Many other subjects deserve this same treatment. For example, it would be valuable to consider the contribution of anarchist pedagogy in a revolutionary reflection on education; we are thinking of the writings of Francisco Ferrer, founder of the Modern School, shot by the Spanish military authorities in 1909 on the false accusation of having instigated the workers' riots in Barcelona; or even of the libertaire Swiss educator Henri Roorda, a young man sponsored by Élisée Reclus, and author of the 1917 satire *Le pédagogue n'aime pas les enfants* (The teacher doesn't like the children).[1]

Another question that we did not broach—except in the historical section—is that of the fight against fascism, the Far Right, and neo-Nazism, for example, in France, in the collectives Ras L'Front, VISA (Vigilance et Initiatives syndicales antifascistes, or Labor Union Antifascist Vigilance and Initiatives), and Action antifasciste; in Greece, against the sinister political party Golden Dawn, and elsewhere. The combativeness and inventiveness of the anarchists in this decisive struggle are undeniable, and the convergences between revolutionary Marxists and libertaires in it have long been evident.

In her *Anthologie libertaire*, Irène Pereira identifies three categories of anarchism: classical anarchism, which is founded on class struggle; libertaire humanism, which establishes humanity as a subject of emancipation; and individualist anarchism.[2] For reasons of historical proximity, we have dealt, in this book, with convergences with the "classist" current (libertaire, anarcho-communist, platformist, anarcho-syndicalist, and so on) without seeking to make them a priori into one.

For us, libertarian Marxism is not a doctrine, not a finished body of theory; it is a matter, rather, of an *affinity*, of a certain political and intellectual approach—the shared desire to do away with, through revolutionary means, the dictatorship of capital in order to build a unalienated, egalitarian society, liberated from the authoritarian shackles of the state. In fact, no one sole libertarian Marxism exists, but rather a wide variety of attempts, more or less successful, at building bridges between the two largest revolutionary traditions. Radicals interested by this approach can be found in anarchist movements like Alternative libertaire (since 2019, Union communiste libertaire), in the libertaire current of the Nouveau Parti anticapitaliste (New Anticapitalist Party), among certain intellectuals close to anarchism (Philippe Corcuff), in radical ecologist circles, or those that conscientiously object to commercial growth (Stéphanie Lavignotte), in aggressive trade unionism (particularly the Italian Syndicalist Union), and in many different social movement and antiracist, antifascist, and anticapitalist networks.

Our point of departure—by way of our particular history and education—is Marxism. It is within this tradition that we have developed an interest in the anarchist experience. But we are convinced that Marxists have much to learn from the thought, culture, struggles, and ideas of the anarchists: their irreconcilable opposition to all forms of tyranny, domination, and oppression; their "radical concept of freedom" (Walter Benjamin); their revolutionary and unyielding spirit, hostile to both capital and the state.[3] We believe that the revolutionary culture of the future, that of twenty-first-century emancipatory struggles, will be both Marxist and anarchist.

If, in regard to some of the questions we have broached, especially in the second part of our book, we defended a position critical of (or in any case, different from that of) the libertaires, it is not because we believe ourselves to have a monopoly on "truth," nor is it out of a conviction of having the most "scientific" analysis. It is quite simply the current state of our thought, as a function of our experience: a provisional state, open to discussion and criticism.

Some time ago, our friends at the Catalan Andreu Nin Foundation organized an event memorializing the seventy-fifth anniversary of the 1937 disappearance of Nin, the Marxist head of the Workers' Party of Unification, and the Italian militant and anarchist thinker Camilo Berneri. Both had come to Barcelona to join the fight against fascism. Their analyses were disparate, their political proposals different, but they were both to be found on the same side of the barricades—that of the great Spanish Revolution. For this, they both paid a heavy price: their assassination by agents of the Stalinist secret police.

We believe—and this book is based on this hope—that the future emancipatory battles of our century will also see this convergence, in both action and thought, of the two great revolutionary currents of the past, of the present, and of the future—Marxism and anarchism, the red flag and the black flag.

M.L. and O.B.

Notes

Foreword

1   Joseph Stalin, *Works*, vol. 1, *November 1901–April 1907* (Moscow: Foreign Languages Publishing House, 1954), accessed June 27, 2022, https://www.marxists.org/reference/archive/stalin/works/1906/12/x01.htm.

The First International and the Paris Commune (1871)

1   [I have kept the French term *libertaire*, which refers to a broad antiauthoritarian revolutionary socialist tendency, because its English equivalent, *libertarian*, has been hijacked by an ultraliberal reactionary capitalist ideology. For more information on this, see pp. xvii–xix.]

2   This information comes from the excellent historical overview by Gaetano Manfredonia, *L'anarchisme en Europe* (Paris: University Press of France, 2001).

3   The General Council of the First International, *Minutes 1868–1870* (Moscow: Progress, 1964), 296, accessed June 27, 2021, https://www.marxists.org/archive/marx/iwma/pdfs/iwma-sep68-jul70.pdf.

4   [The Paris Commune was brutally suppressed by a counterrevolutionary army and government headquartered at Versailles and backed by a broad coalition of essentially all political tendencies except the Far Left.]

5   Mikhail Bakunin, "The Paris Commune and the Idea of the State," in *Bakunin on Anarchy*, ed. Sam Dolgoff (Montreal: Black Rose Books, 2002), 266–67.

6   Karl Marx, "The First Draft of 'The Civil War in France,'" in *The Civil War in France* (Peking: Foreign Languages Press, 1966), 166.

7   Marx, "First Draft," in *Civil War*, 72, 162, 163, 164, 171, 189.

May Day and the Haymarket Martyrs (1886)

1   John P. Altgeld, "Reasons for Pardoning Fielden, Neebe, and Schwab," Famous Trials, accessed June 27, 2022, http://law2.umkc.edu/faculty/projects/ftrials/haymarket/pardon.html.

2   Mark A. Plummer, *Lincoln's Rail Splitter: Governor Richard J. Oglesby* (Urbana: University of Illinois Press, 2001), 196.

3   [For the full text of Lingg's speech, see David Roediger and Franklin Rosemont, eds., *Haymarket Scrapbook* (Chicago: Charles H. Kerr, 1986), 46–47.]

4   All of the above information is taken from Roediger and Rosemont, *Haymarket Scrapbook*.

Revolutionary Trade Unionism and the Charter of Amiens (1906)

1   [*Lois scélérates* or "villainous laws" is a pejorative term used to refer to a series of draconian repressive laws enacted in France in 1893–94 in response to a number of "propaganda-by-the-deed" anarchist attacks.]

2   As property was considered a "theft" by Proudhon, its reappropriation was to occur through "reclamation."

3   [The Sacred Union (French: *Union Sacrée*) was a political agreement in France between the Left and labor organizations and the government, made after the outbreak of World War I, in which the former agreed to support the war effort in the name of patriotism.]

4   [Jean Jaurès (1859–1914) was a reformist French socialist politician who championed participation in government. Jules Guesde (1845–1922) was a revolutionary French socialist politician who rejected participation in government.]

5   Louis-Auguste Blanqui (1805–1881), a leading French revolutionary socialist figure in the nineteenth century, participated actively in the revolutions of 1830 and 1848. His being imprisoned during the Commune in 1871 deprived the revolution of its head, to borrow Karl Marx's words. His ideas gave rise to numerous subversive groups and revolutionary organizations over the course of his life. The many years he spent in prison earned him the nickname L'Enfermé (the Locked-Up One).

6   The Confédération Générale du Travail, "The Charter of Amiens," 1906, trans. Mitch Abidor, accessed June 28, 2022, https://www.marxists.org/history/france/cgt/charter-amiens.htm; emphasis added.

7   The Industrial Workers of the World is a revolutionary international workers union founded in the United States in the same year, 1905. See page 12.

The Spanish Revolution (1936–37): The Red and Black Revolution

1   See "Benjamin Péret" in this volume.
2   Camilo Berneri, *En defensa del POUM* (Madrid: Los Libros de la catarata, 1998).
3   George Orwell, *Homage to Catalonia* (San Diego: Harcourt Brace, 1980), 62.
4   Orwell, *Homage*, 62, 116.
5   For more on the FAI, see "Buenaventura Durruti" in this volume.
6   "Intervention d'Alfred Rosmer à l'occasion de l'hommage international rendu à Andrés Nin (Excerpt from Alfred Rosmer's contribution on the occasion of the international tribute paid to Andrés Nin on June 24th 1954)," *La Battalla*, no. 123, July 25, 1954, quoted in Wilebaldo Soleno, *Le POUM: Révolution dans la guerre d'Espagne* (Paris: Syllepse, 2002), 241.

May 68

1   [Literally, "the events," a common French euphemism for the civil unrest of May 1968.]
2   Daniel Bensaïd and Henri Weber, *Mai 68: Une répétition générale* (Paris: Éditions Maspero, 1968), 101.
3   Daniel Bensaïd, *An Impatient Life: A Memoir*, trans. David Fernbach (London: Verso, 2004), 102.
4   Hervé Hamon and Patrick Rotman, *Génération*, vol. 1, *Les années de rêve* (Paris: Éditions du Seuil, 1987), 431.
5   Hamon and Rotman, *Génération*, 431.
6   Hamon and Rotman, *Génération*, 431.
7   Hamon and Rotman, *Génération*, 432.
8   Bensaïd, *Impatient*, 58.
9   See page 90.
10 Daniel Singer, *Prelude to Revolution: France in May 1968* (Chicago: Haymarket Books, 2013), 357.
11 Singer, *Prelude*, 359.
12 ["Sous les pavés, la plage!" was one of numerous well-known revolutionary slogans created during May 1968, the implication being that people should tear up the paving stones and use them to build barricades. Other slogans included "La barricade ferme la rue mais ouvre la voie" (The barricade blocks the street but opens the way) and "Soyez réalistes, demandez l'impossible" (Be realistic, demand the impossible).]

From Alterglobalization to Occupy Wall Street

1   [ATTAC: Association pour la Taxation des Transactions financière et l'Aide aux Citoyens / Association for the Taxation of Financial Transactions and Aid to Citizens.]

2   Jose Correa Leite, *Forum Social Mundial: A historia de uma invenção politica* (San Paulo: Editora Fundação Perseu Abramo, 2003). [Published in English as *The World Social Forum: Strategies of Resistance* (Chicago: Haymarket Books, 2005).]

3   Dan Bilefsky, "Three Reported Killed in Greek Protests," *New York Times*, May 5, 2010, https://www.nytimes.com/2010/05/06/world/europe/06g reece.html.

4   See page 132.

5   Josep Maria Antentas and Esther Vivas, *Planeta Indignado: Ocupando el futuro* (Madrid: Ediciones Sequitur, 2012), 77.

6   Antentas and Vivas, *Planeta Indignado*, 77.

7   Antentas and Vivas, *Planeta Indignado*, 77.

Letter to Louise Michel (1830–1905)

1   [Adolphe Thiers (1797–1877) and Patrice de MacMahon (1808–1893) were the heads of the Versailles government and army, respectively, and responsible for the brutal suppression of the Commune.]

2   [Neuilly-sur-Seine, a suburb on the western edge of Paris, was the scene of intense street fighting and heavy bombardment by the *versaillais*. Today, it is the most affluent suburb of Paris, home to many celebrities and politicians.]

3   [The Second French Empire collapsed after a humiliating defeat by the Prussians on September 1, 1870, at the very outset of the Franco-Prussian War, in which the emperor himself and more than one hundred thousand troops were captured. When this news reached Paris, elections were called and a new government formed, republican in name but dominated by monarchists and conservatives. It was this government that was later displaced when the Communards seized power, and which went on to become the Third Republic after its suppression of the Commune. The Second Empire had itself displaced the Second Republic some twenty years earlier, a fact which had not been forgotten by the working class. Alistair Horne, in his book *The Terrible Year: The Paris Commune, 1871* describes the long-simmering class conflicts leading up to the declaration of the Commune: "Under the Empire industrial production had doubled.... But somehow, the workers—and more particularly, the Parisian proletariat—had found themselves left out of the general wave of *enrichissez-vous*.... More politically conscious than any other, the Parisian proletariat had never forgiven [the emperor] for destroying the [Second] Republic *they* had created; nor would they forget the

way the *petit bourgeois* had betrayed them.... As indeed previously they felt they had been swindled out of their place in the sun after the uprisings of 1789, 1830 and 1848" (Alistair Horne, *The Terrible Year* [London: Orion Books, 2004], 5–6).]

4 [After their victory at Sédan, the Prussian forces besieged Paris, forcing the new government of the Third Republic to sign an armistice. Once the armistice was signed, there was a massive exodus of the middle and upper classes (and the government itself) from Paris, effectively abandoning the city to the proletariat. Nearby Versailles became the headquarters of the government and army of these classes, led by Adolphe Thiers and Patrice MacMahon. On March 17, the Versailles government sent its troops to retake possession of some two hundred cannons from the Paris National Guard, which was heavily proletarian and radicalized. The National Guard refused to hand over the cannons, and successfully incited many of the soldiers sent to claim them over to their side, sparking the formation of the Commune. Alistair Horne again: "[The] troops were all but submerged by the mob, pouring every kind of seditious argument into their young ears. Suddenly, some were seen to reverse their rifles, raising the butts in the air, accompanied by cries of ... "Down with Thiers!" (Horne, *Terrible*, 73–74).]

5 [The Communards' Wall in Père Lachaise Cemetery in Paris, where the last of the captured Communards were executed by firing squad, is a leftist site of interest, well-known throughout France. Numerous high-profile French leftists have been buried nearby, and the wall itself still bears a large marble slab inscribed "Aux Morts de la Commune" (To the Dead of the Commune).]

6 [Allegedly, the *pétroleuses* were female arsonists who set fire to buildings owned by the wealthy or the government in the last days of the Commune. The existence of *pétroleuses* has been the subject of some debate.]

7 Louise Michel, "The Illegal Candidacy," in *The Red Virgin*, ed. and trans. Bullitt Lowry and Elizabeth Ellington Gunter (Tuscaloosa: University of Alabama Press, 1981), 125.

8 Louise Michel, *Mémoires de Louise Michel écrits par elle-même* (1886), 158, Bibebook, accessed June 28, 2022, http://www.bibebook.com/files/ebook/libre/V2/michel_louise_-_memoires_de_louise_michel_ecrits_par_elle-meme.pdf.]

Pierre Monatte (1881–1960)

1 [Alfred Dreyfus, who was a captain in the French army and of Jewish descent, was convicted in 1894 of passing military secrets to the Germans. Over several years, it was established that he was, in fact, completely innocent. The public debate over the case bitterly

divided French society, generally between the Right and Left, and is today remembered as a massive failing of the French justice system and an example of anti-Semitism at work in France.]

2   *The International Anarchist Congress: Amsterdam, 1907*, trans. Nestor McNab (Federazione dei Comunisti Anarchici, 2007, in pamphlet form), 42–45, accessed June 28, 2022, http://www.fdca.it/fdcaen/historical/amsterdam07/4.htm.

3   [Jean Jaurès was a firm antimilitarist. His assassination destabilized the left antiwar movement in France.]

4   [Léon Jouhaux (1879–1954) was a leading figure within the CGT who encouraged union adherence to the Sacred Union.]

5   Pierre Monatte, *Syndicalisme révolutionnaire et communisme: Les archives de Pierre Monatte* (Paris: Éditions Maspero, 1968), 48–49.

6   Colette Chambelland, "Monatte Pierre, dit Lémont Pierre," Le Maitron, updated July 13, 2020, accessed June 28, 2022, https://maitron.fr/spip.php?article24500.

7   Pierre Monatte to Leon Trotsky, March 13, 1920, trans. Mitchell Abidor, accessed June 28, 2022, https://www.marxists.org/archive/monatte/1920/letter-trotsky.htm.

8   [The Third International (more commonly known as the Comintern) was under the direct control of the Soviet authorities, and was used by them to influence communist movements around the world.]

9   Monatte, *Syndicalisme*, 413.

Rosa Luxemburg (1870–1919)

1   Rosa Luxemburg, "Organizational Question of Social Democracy," in *Rosa Luxemburg Speaks*, ed. Mary-Alice Waters (New York: Pathfinder Press, 1970), 118.

2   Luxemburg, "Organizational Question," 130.

3   Rosa Luxemburg, "The Mass Strike, the Political Party, and the Trade Unions," in *Luxemburg Speaks*, 172.

4   Karl Kautsky, *Der Politische Massenstreik* (Berlin, 1914), 202–3.

5   Rosa Luxemburg, "The Russian Revolution," in *Luxemburg Speaks*, 394.

6   Luxemburg, "Russian Revolution," 389–91.

7   Luxemburg, "Russian Revolution," 392.

8   Luxemburg, "Russian Revolution," 384.

9   Rosa Luxemburg, "Speech to the Founding Convention of the German Communist Party," in *Luxemburg Speaks*, 426–27.

Emma Goldman (1869–1940)

1   Miriam Brody, introduction to Emma Goldman, *Living My Life* (New York: Penguin, 2006), vii.

2   Emma Goldman, *Living My Life*, ed. Miriam Brody (New York: Penguin, 2006), 433.

3   A Russian anarchist, Voline (1882–1945) played an important political role in Nestor Makhno's army in Ukraine from the summer of 1919 onward.

4   Goldman, *Living*, 522.

5   Emma Goldman, *Vision on Fire: Emma Goldman on the Spanish Revolution*, ed. David Porter (Oakland: AK Press, 2006), 167.

Buenaventura Durruti (1896–1936)

1   Abel Paz, *Durruti in the Spanish Revolution*, trans. Chuck Morse (Chico: AK Press, 2007).

2   Paz, *Durruti in the Spanish Revolution*, 5.

3   [Durruti had been conscripted shortly before the August 1917 general strike. "When I left the enlistment office, I declared that Alfonso XIII would have one less soldier and one more revolutionary!" he later wrote. This information from Paz, *Durruti in the Spanish Revolution*, 14.]

4   [There was a rash of bank robberies for individual ends at this time by people who were nonetheless CNT members and who, upon arrest, immediately presented their CNT cards and demanded the organization provide them with legal defense. Durruti argued: "I used those tactics in the past, but times have changed, due to the ascendant march of the CNT and FAI. There are more than one million workers unionized in the CNT—waiting for the right moment to make the great collective expropriation—and they demand a conduct from us that is consistent with the needs of the struggle.... The revolution could explode at any moment.... I think there will be a civil war ... for which we must be well-prepared" (Paz, *Durruti in the Spanish Revolution*, 369–70).]

5   Abel Paz, *Buenaventura Durruti, un combattant libertaire dans la révolution espagnole* (Paris: Éditions de Paris, 2000), 298.

6   Paz, *Durruti in the Spanish Revolution*, 296.

7   Paz, *Buenaventura Durruti*, 331.

8   Mikhail Koltsov quoted in Hans Magnus Enzensberger, *Anarchy's Brief Summer*, trans. Mike Mitchell (London: Seagull, 2018), 224–25.

9   Paz, *Durruti in the Spanish Revolution*, 474.

10 Leon Trotsky, "The Lessons of Spain: The Last Warning," in *Socialist Appeal* 2, no. 2 (January 8, 1938): 4–5; continued in *Socialist Appeal* no. 3 (January 15, 1938): 4–5, 8, accessed June 29, 2022, https://www.marxists.org/archive/trotsky/1937/xx/spain01.htm.

Benjamin Péret (1899–1959)

1   All quotes in this section are from Benjamin Péret, *La Commune des Palmares* (Paris: Éditions Syllepse, 1999).

Subcomandante Marcos (1957–)

1   Subcomandante Marcos, "'A Political Force in Formation': Is this Some Kind of Joke?" in *Shadows of Tender Fury: The Letters and Communiqués of Subcomandante Marcos and the Zapatista Army of National Liberation*, trans. Frank Bardacke, Leslie Lopez, and the Watsonville, California, Human Rights Committee (New York: Monthly Review Press, 1995), 108.

2   Jérôme Baschet, *La Rébellion Zapatiste: Insurrection indienne, résistance planétaire* (Paris: Éditions Flammarion, 2005), 30.

3   Baschet, Rébellion, 65.

4   Baschet, Rébellion, 65–67, 89.

The Russian Revolution (1917–20)

1   Leon Trotsky, *History of the Russian Revolution*, trans. Max Eastman (Chicago: Haymarket Books, 2008), 13.

2   Daniel Guérin, *Anarchism: From Theory to Practice*, trans. Mary Klopper (New York: Monthly Review Press, 1970), 82.

3   Guérin, *Anarchism*, 85.

4   V.I. Lenin, *The State and Revolution*, ed. Todd Chretien (Chicago: Haymarket Books, 2014).

5   Signed in March 1918 by Russia (the Russian Soviet Federative Socialist Republic) and the governments of the Central Powers (notably the Reich), the treaty brought an end to the fighting on the Eastern Front at the cost of a significant loss of Russian territory, and de facto implied Soviet Russia's neutrality toward the Finnish Revolution, then underway.

6   [This refers to Imperial Russia's allies in World War I. With the Treaty of Brest-Litovsk, the Bolsheviks ended these alliances and withdrew Russia from the war. However, several of these former allies subsequently invaded Russia in support of the Whites. As historian S.A. Smith explains, "The civil war had international ramifications, initially in relation to the outcome of the First World War, later in relation to the carving out of post-war spheres of influence." Smith, *The Russian Revolution: A Very Short Introduction* (NY: Oxford University Press, 2002), 48.]

7   Victor Serge, "Thirty Years After the Russian Revolution," in *Russia Twenty Years After*, ed. Susan Weissman (New Jersey: Humanities, 1996), 312.

8   Victor Serge, *Memoirs of a Revolutionary*, trans. Peter Sedgwick with George Paizis (New York: New York Review Books, 2012), 140.

9   See "Nestor Makhno," in this volume.
10 Peter Kropotkin (1842–1921) was an anarchist of international renown whose funeral in Moscow on February 8, 1921, was a massive demonstration, the last act of defiance of the anarchists against the Bolshevik authorities.
11 [The Black Guards were anarchist workers' militias.]
12 Emma Goldman, *Living My Life*, ed. Miriam Brody (New York: Penguin, 2006), 422.
13 ["White Guards" was a general term for partisans of the "White" anti-Bolshevik movement during the civil war.]
14 Serge, *Memoirs*, 139.
15 [Commissariats were state administrative bodies in the Soviet Union, comparable to ministries.]
16 Serge, *Memoirs*, 110.
17 Serge, *Memoirs*, 141.
18 *Thermidor* was a month in the French revolutionary calendar. On Thermidor 10, 1794 (July 28), Robespierre and his associate Saint-Just were overthrown and executed, and a right-wing bourgeois republican group took power. It was the end of the French Revolution as a left-wing movement. According to Trotsky, Stalin's hegemony in the Soviet Union during the 1920s was a sort of Thermidor of the Russian Revolution.
19 Leon Trotsky, "The Errors in Principle of Syndicalism," *Militant* 3, no. 7 (February 15, 1930): 4, accessed June 30, 2022, https://www.marxists.org/archive/trotsky/1931/unions/4-errors.htm.
20 Leon Trotsky, "Stalinism and Bolshevism," in *Socialist Appeal* 1, no. 7 (September 25, 1937): 4–5; no. 8 (October 2, 1937): 4–5, accessed June 30, 2022, https://www.marxists.org/archive/trotsky/1937/08/stalinism.htm.
21 Daniel Guérin, "La Question que Trotsky ne pose pas," in *À la recherche d'un communisme libertaire* (Paris: Éditions Spartacus, 1984).
22 Karl Marx, "Address of the General Council of the International," in *The Civil War in France* (Peking: Foreign Languages Press, 1966), 72.
23 Trotsky, *History*, 860.

Revisiting the Kronstadt Tragedy

1   Paul Avrich, *Kronstadt, 1921* (Princeton: Princeton, 1970), 162.
2   Emma Goldman, *Living My Life*, ed. Miriam Brody (New York: Penguin, 2006), 503–4.
3   "What We Are Fighting For," *Izvestia*, March 8, 1921, quoted in Avrich, *Kronstadt*, 243.
4   Georges Fontenis and Alexandre Skirda, eds., *1921, L'insurrection de Cronstadt la rouge: Le pouvoir des soviets libres*, 5th ed. (Paris:

Ed. Alternative libertaire, 2008). Alternative libertaire, now part of the Union communiste libertaire, was an anarchist organization founded in 1991 with a small publishing company producing a magazine of the same name, as well as a number of booklets and pamphlets, such as this one.

5   V.I. Lenin, "The Lessons of Kronstadt," in *Kronstadt*, by V.I. Lenin and Leon Trotsky, ed. Barbara Mutnick (New York: Pathfinder Press, 1979), 58.

6   V.I. Lenin, "Report on the Substitution of a Tax in Kind for the Surplus-Grain Appropriation System, March 15," in *Collected Works*, ed. and trans. Yuri Sdobnikov (Moscow: Progress Publishers, 1973), 32:228.

7   Trotsky, "Comments to the Foreign Press," in Lenin and Trotsky, *Kronstadt*, 89–90.

8   Trotsky, "The Questions of Wendelin Thomas," in Lenin and Trotsky, *Kronstadt*, 103.

9   Trotsky, "A Tragic Necessity," in Lenin and Trotsky, *Kronstadt*, 127.

10 Avrich, *Kronstadt*, 139.

11 Alexander Berkman, *The Kronstadt Rebellion* (Berlin: Der Sindikalist, 1922), accessed June 30, 2022, https://www.marxists.org/reference/archive/berkman/1922/kronstadt-rebellion/afterword.htm.

12 Patrice Spadoni, "Kronstadt, ou la tragique erreur de Lénine et Trotsky" in Fontenis and Skirda, *1921, L'insurrection*.

13 [Gaston Alexandre Auguste, Marquis de Gallifet (1830–1909) was a French general known as le Fusilleur de la Commune (the executioner of the Commune) for his central role in the bloody suppression of the Paris Commune in 1871.]

14 Spadoni, "Kronstadt, ou la tragique erreur," in Fontenis and Skirda, *L'insurrection*, 8; Mouvement Communiste Libertaire, "Cronstadt, point de non-retour de la revolution proletarienne," in Fontenis and Skirda, *L'insurrection*, 13, 16–17.

15 [The Bonnot Gang was an illegalist, French anarchist gang that carried out a series of highly publicized thefts and robberies in 1911–12.]

16 Trotsky, "Questions," in Lenin and Trotsky, *Kronstadt*,103.

17 [As George Saunders, who translated "a long footnote on Kronstadt that appears in Trotsky's *Sochineniya* (*Collected Works*)," explains: "These were barrier units, or armed detachments of the Soviet government operating on the outskirts of cities to prevent unauthorized trade during the civil war; in this case, they prevented Petrograd workers from taking manufactured goods out into the neighboring countryside to barter for food, and confiscated food products from those trying to bring them into the city without authorization" (Lenin and Trotsky, *Kronstadt*, 10). For contrast, see

Alexander Berkman's explanation: "Armed units organized by the Bolsheviki for the purpose of suppressing traffic and confiscating foodstuffs and other products. The irresponsibility and arbitrariness of their methods were proverbial throughout the country" (Berkman, *Kronstadt Rebellion*), https://theanarchistlibrary.org/library/alexander-berkman-the-kronstadt-rebellion)].

18   Victor Serge, extract from "Fiction and Fact: Kronstadt," in *The Serge-Trotsky Papers*, ed. D.J. Cotterill (London: Pluto Press, 1994), 163–64.

19   Serge, "Fiction and Fact," 164.

20   Serge, "Fiction and Fact," 164.

21   Serge, "Fiction and Fact," 165.

22   Victor Serge, *Memoirs of a Revolutionary*, trans. Peter Sedgwick and George Paiszis (New York: New York Review of Books, 2012), 150.

23   Serge, *Memoirs*, 150–51.

24   Avrich, *Kronstadt*, 6.

25   Trotsky, "Tragic Necessity," in Lenin and Trotsky, *Kronstadt*, 127.

26   [Trotsky, in order to counter the fact that the Kronstadt sailors had played a pivotal role in the October Revolution, spread the false allegation that all of the sailors who had participated in the revolution had, by the time of the Kronstadt Rebellion, been rotated out and others rotated in, the implication being that the sailors who rose up against the Bolsheviks were not the same ones who helped them win the revolution.]

27   Yves Ternon, *Makhno: La révolte anarchiste* (Brussels: Éditions Complexe, 1981).

28   Serge, *Memoirs*, 140.

29   Nestor Makhno, "Visit to the Kremlin," in *No Gods No Masters: An Anthology of Anarchism*, ed. Daniel Guérin, trans. Paul Sharkey (Oakland: AK Press, 2005), 510, 512.

30   Makhno, "Visit," 510.

31   Serge, *Memoirs*, 142.

32   Serge, *Memoirs*, 142.

33   The treaty can be summed up as follows: "The Insurrectionary Revolutionary Army [Makhnovtsi] would join with the Red Army, but would not be answerable to it, save from a strictly military point of view; it had the right to the same provisions of foodstuffs and munitions; it kept its name, its black flag, and its structure (voluntary association, electoral participation, self-discipline). Moreover, it would accept no political power (commissars) in the region in which it maneuvered. The Bolsheviks accepted, thinking they could later absorb the Makhnovtsi" (Pascal Nurnberg, "Nestor Makhno et l'Armée insurrectionnelle d'Ukraine," *Le Monde libertaire*, December 9–15, 2010).

34   Serge, *Memoirs*, 181.

35   [The authors later cite sociologist Irène Pereira's definition of liber-
     taire humanism as a tendency of anarchism that "establishes human-
     ity as a subject of emancipation," distinct from class-struggle anar-
     chism and individualist anarchism. See page 158.
36   Group of Russian Anarchists Abroad, "The Organizational Platform
     of the General Union of Anarchists," *Dielo Truda*, 1926, June 30, 2022,
     http://www.nestormakhno.info/english/newplatform/org_plat.
     htm.

Walter Benjamin (1894–1940)

1   Walter Benjamin, "The Life of Students," in *Early Writings (1910–
     1917)*, ed. and trans. Howard Eiland, (Cambridge: Harvard University
     Press, 2011), 197.
2   Benjamin, "Students," 201, 203.
3   Walter Benjamin, "Critique of Violence," in *Reflections: Essays,
     Aphorisms, Autobiographical Writings*, ed. Peter Demetz, trans.
     Edmund Jephcott (New York: Schocken Books, 1978), 287, 288.
4   Benjamin, "Critique," 288, 291.
5   Benjamin, "Critique," 292.
6   Walter Benjamin, "The Right to Use Force," in *Selected Writings*, vol. 1:
     1913–1926, ed. Marcus Bullock and Michael W. Jennings (Cambridge:
     Harvard University Press, 1996), 233.
7   Benjamin, "One-Way Street," in *Selected Writings*, 1:430.
8   Walter Benjamin, "Surrealism: The Last Snapshot of the European
     Intelligentsia," in *Reflections*, 177.
9   Benjamin, "Surrealism," 180.
10   Benjamin, "Surrealism," 187. Although Rimbaud and Lautréamont
     were among those recognized as their precursors by the surreal-
     ists, this does not seem to be the case for Dostoyevsky, except for
     Max Ernst, who depicted him in his famous 1921 painting, *A Friends'
     Reunion*.
11   Benjamin, "Surrealism," 188.
12   The German word "Spiesser" is a heavily charged one that refers
     to the crude, narrow-minded, and prosaic individual of bourgeois
     society. Cf. Walter Benjamin, "Der Surrealismus," in *Gesammelte
     Schriften* (Frankfurt: Suhrkamp Verlag, 1985), 2:305.
13   Benjamin, "Surrealism," 187.
14   Benjamin, "Surrealism," 189.
15   [The Rif War was a brutal Spanish colonial counterinsurgency con-
     flict in Morocco from 1921 to 1926. France joined in on the Spanish
     side in 1925.]
16   Benjamin, "Surrealism," 185.
17   Benjamin, "Surrealism," 189.

18   Benjamin, "Surrealism," 189. Benjamin also asks if the surrealists have "bound revolt to revolution."

19   Rolf Tiedemann, epilogue to Walter Benjamin, *Charles Baudelaire: Ein Lyriker im Zeitalter des Hochkapitalismus* (Frankfurt: Suhrkamp Verlag, 1980), 207.

20   Rolf Tiedemann, "Historical Materialism or Political Messianism?" in *Benjamin: Philosophy, History, Aesthetics*, ed. Gary Smith, trans. Barton Byg, Jeremy Gaines, and Doris L. Jones. (Chicago: University of Chicago Press, 1983), 200.

André Breton (1896–1966)

1   André Breton, et al., *Au Grand Jour* (Paris: Éditions Surréalistes, 1927).

2   André Breton, "Second Manifesto of Surrealism," in *Manifestoes of Surrealism*, trans. Richard Seaver and Helen R. Lane (Ann Arbor: University of Michigan press, 1969), 142.

3   Breton, "Second Manifesto," 149.

4   André Breton, "Manifesto of Surrealism," in *Manifestoes of Surrealism*, 4.

5   Maurice Nadeau, "Du temps que les surréalistes avaient raison," in *Documents surréalistes* (Paris: Éditions du Seuil, 1948), 309.

6   André Breton and Diego Rivera, "Manifesto for an Independent Revolutionary Art," July 25, 1938, accessed June 30, 2022, https://www.marxists.org/subject/art/lit_crit/works/rivera/manifesto.htm.

7   André Breton, "To the Lighthouse," trans. Doug Imrie, Michael William, and John P. Clark, in *Anarchism: A Documentary History of Libertarian Ideas*, ed. Robert Graham (Montreal: Black Rose Books, 2009), 2:128.

8   Breton, "Lighthouse," 2:130.

9   For more information on this period, see the two excellent pamphlets published under the title *Surréalisme et Anarchisme* by the Atélier de Création libertaire de Lyon in 1992 and 1994.

10   Arturo Schwarz, *Breton/Trotsky* (Paris: Union générale d'éditions, 1977), 194.

11   Schwarz, *Breton/Trotsky*, 194. [Louis de Saint-Just (1767–1794) was a young Jacobin leader in the French Revolution and a close associate of Robespierre. They were both arrested and executed in the month of Thermidor in the French Revolutionary calendar.]

12   Schwarz, *Breton/Trotsky*, 200.

Daniel Guérin (1904–1988)

1   Daniel Guérin, preface to *À la recherche d'un communisme libertaire* (Paris: Éditions Spartacus, 1984).

2   Guérin, preface.
3   Guérin, preface.
4   Daniel Guérin, *Frères jumeaux, frères ennemis* (Paris: Éditions Spartacus, 1966), 18.
5   Guérin, *Frères*, 18.
6   Guérin, *Frères*, 18.
7   Guérin, *Frères*, 18.
8   Daniel Guérin, "A Libertarian Marx?" 1969(?), accessed June 30, 2022, https://www.marxists.org/history/etol/writers/guerin/19xx/xx/libmarx.html.
9   Guérin, *Frères*, 19.
10 Taken from his lecture in New York, November 1973, in Daniel Guérin, *L'Anarchisme* (Paris: Éditions Gallimard, 1981), 252.
11 Daniel Guérin quoted in "Daniel Guérin: Anarchism Reconsidered," in *Anarchism: A Documentary History of Libertarian Ideas*, ed. Robert Graham (Montreal: Black Rose Books, 2009), 2:282.

Individual and Collective

1   Max Stirner, *The Ego and Its Own*, ed. David Leopold (Cambridge: Cambridge University Press, 1995), 143.
2   Daniel Guérin, *Anarchism: From Theory to Practice*, trans. Mary Klopper (New York: Monthly Review Press, 1970), 33.
3   Karl Marx, *Economic and Philosophic Manuscripts of 1844* (Moscow: Progress Publishers, 1977), 100.
4   Marx, *Economic and Philosophic Manuscripts*, 94.
5   Ernesto Guevara, "On the Budgetary Finance System," in *Che Guevara Reader: Writings on Politics and Revolution*, ed. David Deutschmann (North Melbourne: Ocean Press, 2003), 208, 209.
6   Ernesto Guevara, "Socialism and Man in Cuba," in *Che Guevara Reader*, 244, 248.
7   Guevara, "Socialism and Man," 238.
8   Ernesto Guevara, "A Party of the Working Class," in *Che Guevara Reader*, 199.
9   Philippe Corcuff, Jacques Ion, and François de Singly, *Politiques de L'individualisme* (Paris: Éditions Textuel, 2005).
10 Auguste Blanqui, "Communism, the Future of Society," in *The Blanqui Reader: Political Writings 1830–1880*, ed. Philippe Le Goff and Peter Hallward, trans. Philippe Le Goff, Peter Hallward, and Mitchell Abidor (London: Verso Books, 2018), 277.
11 Blanqui, "Communism," 278.
12 Jacques Rancière, *The Ignorant Schoolmaster: Five Lessons in Intellectual Emancipation*, trans. Kristin Ross (Stanford: Stanford University Press, 1991).

13 Jacques Rancière, *Dissenting Words: Interviews with Jacques Rancière*, ed. and trans. Emiliano Battista (London: Bloomsbury Academic, 2017).

14 [This footnote appears in the English translation of *Hatred of Democracy:* "In 1815, the Bourbon Restoration restricted the franchise to those able to afford a *cens* (fee) of 300 francs. *Un censitaire* is used in the sense of an elector able to pay the *cens*."]

15 Jacques Rancière, *Hatred of Democracy*, trans. Steve Corcoran (New York: Verso Books, 2006), 28.

16 François de Singly, "Pour un socialisme individualiste," in *Politiques de l'individualisme*, ed. Philippe Corcuff, Jacques Ion, and François de Singly (Paris: Éditions Textuel, 2005), 123.

Making Revolution without Taking Power?

1 John Holloway, *Change the World without Taking Power* (London: Pluto Press, 2005).

2 Holloway, *Change*, 92.

3 Karl Marx, *The Civil War in France* (Peking: Foreign Languages Press, 1966), 69–71.

4 See page 57 and following.

5 Holloway, *Change*, 105.

6 See page 76 and following.

7 Anton Pannekoek, "The Proletarian Revolution," in *Lenin as Philosopher* (1938), accessed July 4, 2022, https://www.marxists.org/archive/pannekoe/1938/lenin/ch08.htm

Autonomy and Federalism

1 [Ernest Mandel (1923–1995) was a Belgian Trotskyist economist, theorist, and leader of the Fourth International.]

Democratic Economic Planning and Self-Management

1 Ernest Mandel, *Contrôle ouvrier, conseils ouvriers, autogestion: Anthologie* (Paris, Éditions Maspero, 1973), 6. The principal weakness of the anthology is the absence of anarchist texts. In the preface (to the original French edition), Mandel debates the anarchists with a very dubious argument: "The fundamental tendency of technology is toward centralization" (32). This is less and less the case, but in any event, technology is not independent of social and political changes.

2 [French watchmaking company LIP was the subject of a highly publicized labor struggle including strikes and ultimately workers' self-management in 1973. *The Take* documents the implementation of a workers' cooperative at an auto factory in Buenos Aires, Argentina.]

3   [Deuxième Gauche describes a type of French social-democratic
      movement that attempts to distinguish itself from the "first Left" of
      Marxism. Michel Rocard, a principal figure within this tendency,
      was in fact one of the founding members of the Deuxième Gauche
      as an opposition group within the Confédération française démocra-
      tique du travail (CFDT; French Democratic Confederation of Labor)
      in 1974. The CFDT is one of five major labor union coalitions and
      since the 1970s it has moved away from workers' self-management
      and hardline Marxist principles.]
4   Nelson Méndez and Alfredo Vallota, "Une perspective anarchiste de
      l'autogestion," in L'autogestion anarchiste (Paris: Éditions du monde
      libertaire, 2006), 27. [Fédération anarchiste is a French anarchist
      organization founded in 1945.]
5   Méndez and Vallota, "Perspective anarchiste," 27.
6   Ernest Mandel, Power and Money: A Marxist Theory of Bureaucracy
      (London: Verso, 1992), 204.
7   Michael Albert, Moving Forward: Program for a Participatory
      Economy (San Francisco: AK, 2000), 89.
8   Albert, Forward, 90.

Direct and Representative Democracy

1   Michael Bakunin, "Representative System Based on Fiction," in
      The Political Philosophy of Bakunin: Scientific Anarchism, ed. G.P.
      Maximoff (London: Free Press of Glencoe, 1953), 220.

Union and Party

1   ["Kanaky" is the Indigenous name for the former colony and current
      overseas collectivity of France in the South Pacific also known as
      New Caledonia.]
2   [Sud is an acronym for "solidaric, unified, democratic." The Sud-
      Solidaires unions are a coalition of French trade unions with
      generally far-left politics. They are often associated with the New
      Anticapitalist Party.]
3   Luxemburg, "The Russian Revolution," in Rosa Luxemburg Speaks,
      ed. Mary-Alice Waters (New York: Pathfinder Press, 1970), 389.
4   Luxemburg, The Mass Strike, in Luxemburg Speaks, 163, 207.
5   Anton Pannekoek, Workers' Councils, ed. Robert F. Barsky
      (Edinburgh: AK Press, 2003).
6   Georg Lukács, "Legality and Illegality" in History and Class
      Consciousness, trans. Rodney Livingstone (London: Merlin Press, 1967),
      accessed July 4, 2022, https://www.marxists.org/archive/lukacs/
      works/history/ch06.htm.

Ecosocialism and Anarchist Ecology

1   Murray Bookchin, *Toward an Ecological Society* (Montreal: Black Rose Books, 1980).
2   Bookchin, *Ecological*, 58, 66.
3   Bookchin, *Ecological*, 66.
4   Bookchin, *Ecological*, 68.
5   Such as, we might add, the failed Notre-Dame-des-Landes airport project. [The ZAD, made famous worldwide by the French state's attempts to evict it in 2018, arose in opposition to this "large, useless project."]
6   Bookchin, *Ecological*, 26.
7   Bookchin, *Ecological*, 256.
8   Murray Bookchin, *Post-Scarcity Anarchism* (Montreal: Black Rose Books, 1986), 123.
9   Bookchin, *Post-Scarcity*, 12.
10 Bookchin, *Post-Scarcity*, 44.
11 Bookchin, *Ecological*, 92, 99.
12 Bookchin, *Ecological*, 43, 45, 141.
13 Bookchin, *Post-Scarcity*, 134.
14 Bookchin, *Post-Scarcity*, 159.
15 Bookchin, *Ecological*, 66.
16 Bookchin, *Post-Scarcity*, 112. This is Bookchin's weakest and most debatable essay.

Toward a Libertarian Marxism

1   Republished by Mille et une nuits in "La Petite Collection," 2012.
2   Irène Pereira, *L'anarchisme dans les textes—Anthologie libertaire* (Paris: Textuel, 2011).
3   Walter Benjamin, "Surrealism: The Last Snapshot of the European Intelligentsia," in *Reflections: Essays, Aphorisms, Autobiographical Writings*, ed. Peter Demetz, trans. Edmund Jephcott (New York: Schocken Books, 1978), 189.

Selected Bibliography

Albert, Michael. *Moving Forward: Program for a Participatory Economy.* San Francisco: AK Press, 2000.

Altgeld, John P. "The Pardon of the Haymarket Prisoners (June 26, 1893)." Famous Trials. Accessed December 12, 2022, http://law2.umkc.edu/faculty/projects/ftrials/haymarket/pardon.html.

Antentas, Josep Maria, and Esther Vivas. *Planeta Indignado: Ocupando el futuro.* Madrid: Sequitur, 2012.

Aragon, Louis, André Breton, Paul Éluard, Benjamin Péret, and Pierre Unik. *Au Grand Jour.* Paris: Éditions Surréalistes, 1927.

Atélier de Création libertaire de Lyon. *Surréalisme et anarchisme,* Collection "Le Miroir noir." No. 1, 1992. Accessed December 12, 2022, http://www.atelierdecreationlibertaire.com/Surrealisme-et-anarchisme.html.

Avrich, Paul. *Kronstadt, 1921.* Princeton, NJ: Princeton University Press, 1970.

Bakunin, Michael. *God and the State.* New York: Dover Publications, 1970.

——. "The Paris Commune and the Idea of the State." In *Bakunin on Anarchy,* edited by Sam Dolgoff, 259–73. Montreal: Black Rose Books, 2002.

Baschet, Jérôme. *La Rébellion Zapatiste: Insurrection indienne, résistance planétaire.* Paris: Éditions Flammarion, 2005.

Benjamin, Walter. "Critique of Violence." In *Reflections: Essays, Aphorisms, Autobiographical Writings.* Edited by Peter Demetz. Translated by Edmund Jephcott. New York: Schocken Books, 1978.

——. "Der Surrealismus: Die letzte Momentaufnahme der europäischen Intelligenz." In *Gesammelte Schriften,* vol. 2. Frankfurt: Suhrkamp Verlag, 1985.

——. "The Life of Students." In *Early Writings (1910–1917),* edited and translated by Howard Eiland, 197–210. Cambridge, MA: Harvard University Press, 2011.

———. "On the Concept of History." In *Selected Writings*, vol. 4, *1938–1940*, edited by Marcus Bullock and Michael W. Jennings, 389–400. Cambridge, MA: Harvard University Press, 1996.

———. "One-Way Street." In *Selected Writings*, vol. 1, *1913–1926*, edited by Marcus Bullock and Michael W. Jennings, 444–88. Cambridge, MA: Harvard University Press, 1996.

———. "The Right to Use Force." In *Selected Writings*, vol. 1, *1913–1926*, edited by Marcus Bullock and Michael W. Jennings, 231–34. Cambridge, MA: Harvard University Press, 1996.

———. "Surrealism: The Last Snapshot of the European Intelligentsia." In *Reflections: Essays, Aphorisms, Autobiographical Writings*, edited by Peter Demetz, translated by Edmund Jephcott, 47–56. New York: Schocken Books, 1978.

Bensaïd, Daniel. *An Impatient Life: A Memoir*. Translated by David Fernbach. London: Verso, 2004.

Bensaïd, Daniel, and Henri Weber. *Mai 68: Une répétition générale*. Paris: Maspero, 1968.

Berneri, Camilo. "En defensa del POUM." In *Humanismo y Anarquismo*, edited by Ernest Cañada. Madrid: Los Libros de la catarata, 1998.

Berkman, Alexander. *The Kronstadt Rebellion*. Berlin: Der Sindikalist, 1922. Accessed December 17, 2022. https://www.marxists.org/reference/archive/berkman/1922/kronstadt-rebellion/index.htm.

Blanqui, Auguste. "Communism, the Future of Society." In *The Blanqui Reader: Political Writings 1830–1880*. Edited by Philippe Le Goff and Peter Hallward. Translated by Philippe Le Goff, Peter Hallward, and Mitchell Abidor. London: Verso Books, 2018.

Bookchin, Murray. "Ecology and Revolutionary Thought." In *Post-Scarcity Anarchism*. Montreal: Black Rose Books, 1986.

———. *Toward an Ecological Society*. Montreal: Black Rose Books, 1980.

Breton, André. "Manifesto of Surrealism." In Breton, *Manifestoes of Surrealism*.

———. *Manifestoes of Surrealism*. Translated by Richard Seaver and Helen R. Lane. Ann Arbor: University of Michigan Press, 1969.

———. "Second Manifesto of Surrealism." In Breton, *Manifestoes of Surrealism*.

———. "To the Lighthouse." In *Anarchism: A Documentary History of Libertarian Ideas*, vol. 2, *The Emergence of the New Anarchism (1939–1977)*, edited by Robert Graham. Montreal: Black Rose Books, 2009.

Breton, André, and Diego Rivera. "Manifesto for an Independent Revolutionary Art." Accessed December 17, 2022. https://www.marxists.org/subject/art/lit_crit/works/rivera/manifesto.htm.

Chambelland, Colette. "Monatte Pierre, dit Lémont Pierre." Le Maitron, updated September 12, 2022. Accessed December 17, 2022. https://maitron.fr/spip.php?article24500.

Confédération Générale du Travail. "The Charter of Amiens." Translated by Mitch Abidor. Accessed December 17, 2022. https://www.marxists.org/history/france/cgt/charter-amiens.htm.

Corcuff, Philippe, Jacques Ion, and François de Singly. *Politiques de L'individualisme*. Paris: Éditions Textuel, 2005.

Cotterill, D.J., ed. *The Serge-Trotsky Papers*. London: Pluto Press, 1994.

Enzensberger, Hans Magnus. *Anarchy's Brief Summer*. Translated by Mike Mitchell. London: Seagull Books, 2018.

Fontenis, Georges, and Alexandre Skirda, eds. *1921, L'insurrection de Cronstadt la rouge: Le pouvoir des soviets libres*. 5th ed. Paris: Éditions Alternative libertaire, 2008.

General Council of the First International. *Minutes 1868–1870*. Moscow: Progress Publishers, 1964. Accessed December 17, 2022. https://www.marxists.org/archive/marx/iwma/pdfs/iwma-sep68-jul70.pdf.

Goldman, Emma. *Living My Life*. Edited by Miriam Brody. New York: Penguin, 2006.

———. *Vision on Fire: Emma Goldman on the Spanish Revolution*. Edited by David Porter. Oakland: AK Press, 2006.

Group of Russian Anarchists Abroad. "The Organizational Platform of the General Union of Anarchists." Accessed December 17, 2022. http://www.nestormakhno.info/english/newplatform/org_plat.htm.

Guérin, Daniel. *Anarchism: From Theory to Practice*. Translated by Mary Klopper. New York: Monthly Review Press, 1970.

———. *Anarchism Reconsidered*. In *Anarchism: A Documentary History of Libertarian Ideas*, vol. 2, *The Emergence of the New Anarchism (1939–1977)*, edited by Robert Graham. Montreal: Black Rose Books, 2009.

———. *Frères jumeaux, frères ennemis*. Paris: Éditions Spartacus, 1966.

———. *L'Anarchisme*. Paris: Éditions Gallimard, 1981.

———. "La Question que Trotsky ne pose pas." In *À la recherche d'un communisme libertaire*. Paris: Éditions Spartacus, 1984.

———. "A Libertarian Marx?" Accessed December 17, 2022. https://www.marxists.org/history/etol/writers/guerin/19xx/xx/libmarx.html.

———. *Rosa Luxemburg et la spontanéité révolutionnaire*. Paris: Éditions Spartacus, 1971.

Guevara, Ernesto. "On the Budgetary Finance System." In *Che Guevara Reader: Writings on Politics and Revolution*. Edited by David Deutschmann. North Melbourne: Ocean Press, 2003.

Hamon, Hervé, and Patrick Rotman. *Génération*, vol. 1, *Les Années de Rêve*. Paris: Éditions du Seuil, 1987.

Holloway, John. *Change the World without Taking Power*. London: Pluto Press, 2005.

International Anarchist Congress: Amsterdam, 1907. Translated by Nestor McNab. Federazione dei Comunisti Anarchici. Accessed December 12, 2022, http://www.fdca.it/fdcaen/historical/amsterdam07/4.htm.

Izvestia. "What We Are Fighting For," March 8, 1921. In Avrich, *Kronstadt, 1921*, 241–43.

Kautsky, Karl. *Der Politische Massenstreik*. Berlin, 1914. Accessed December 17, 2022. https://www.marxists.org/deutsch/archiv/kautsky/1914/genstreik/index.html.

Leite, José Correa. *Forum Social Mundial: A historia de uma invenção politica*. São Paulo: Editora Fundação Perseu Abramo, 2003.

———. *The World Social Forum: Strategies of Resistance*. Chicago: Haymarket Books, 2005.

Lenin, V.I. "Report on the Substitution of a Tax in Kind for the Surplus-Grain Appropriation System, March 15." In *Collected Works*, vol. 23. Edited and translated by Yuri Sdobnikov. Moscow: Progress Publishers, 1973.

———. *The State and Revolution*. Edited by Todd Chretien. Chicago: Haymarket Books, 2014.

Lenin, V.I., and Leon Trotsky. *Kronstadt*. Edited by Barbara Mutnick. New York: Pathfinder Press, 1979.

Lewis, Avi, dir. *The Take*. Toronto: Barna-Alper Productions. 2004. Accessed December 12, 2022. https://www.youtube.com/watch?v=3-DSu8RPJt8.

Lukács, Georg. "Legality and Illegality." In *History and Class Consciousness*. Translated by Rodney Livingstone. London: Merlin Press, 1967. Accessed December 12, 2022. https://www.marxists.org/archive/lukacs/works/history/ch06.htm.

Luxemburg, Rosa. "The Mass Strike, the Political Party, and the Trade Unions." In *Rosa Luxemburg Speaks*.

———. "Organizational Question of Social Democracy." In *Rosa Luxemburg Speaks*.

———. *Rosa Luxemburg Speaks*. Edited by Mary-Alice Waters. New York: Pathfinder Press, 1970.

———. "The Russian Revolution." In *Rosa Luxemburg Speaks*.

———. "Speech to the Founding Convention of the German Communist Party." In *Rosa Luxemburg Speaks*.

Makhno, Nestor. "Visit to the Kremlin." In *No Gods No Masters: An Anthology of Anarchism*. Edited by Daniel Guérin. Translated by Paul Sharkey. Oakland: AK Press, 2005.

Mandel, Ernest. *Contrôle ouvrier, conseils ouvriers, autogestion: Anthologie*. Paris: François Maspero, coll. "Poche rouge," 1973.

———. *Power and Money: A Marxist Theory of Bureaucracy*. London: Verso, 1992.

———. "Workers' Control and Workers' Councils." *International* 2, no. 1 (1973). Accessed December 12, 2022. https://www.marxists.org/archive/mandel/1973/xx/wcwc.html#f21.

Manfredonia, Gaetano. *L'anarchisme en Europe*. Paris: Presses Universitaires de France, 2001.

Marcos, Subcomandante. "'A Political Force in Formation': Is this Some Kind of Joke?" In *Shadows of Tender Fury: The Letters and Communiqués of Subcomandante Marcos and The Zapatista Army of National Liberation*, translated by Frank Bardacke, Leslie Lopez, and the Watsonville, California, Human Rights Committee. New York: Monthly Review Press, 1995.

Marx, Karl. "Address of the General Council of the International." In *The Civil War in France*. Peking: Foreign Languages Press, 1966.

———. *Capital*. Translated by David Fernbach. 3 vols. London: Penguin Classics, 1992.

———. *The Civil War in France*. Peking: Foreign Languages Press, 1966.

———. *Economic and Philosophic Manuscripts of 1844*. Moscow: Progress Publishers, 1977.

———. "The First Draft of 'the Civil War in France.'" In *The Civil War in France*. Peking: Foreign Languages Press, 1966.

Méndez, Nelson, and Alfredo Vallota. "Une perspective anarchiste de l'autogestion." In *L'autogestion anarchiste*. Paris: Éditions du monde libertaire, 2006.

Mett, Ida. "The Kronstadt Commune." In *Solidarity Pamphlet No. 27, November 1967*. Accessed December 12, 2022. https://www.marxists.org/archive/mett/1938/kronstadt.htm.

Michel, Louise. "The Illegal Candidacy." In *The Red Virgin*. Edited and translated by Bullitt Lowry and Elizabeth Ellington Gunter. Tuscaloosa: University of Alabama Press, 1981.

———. *Mémoires de Louise Michel écrits par elle-même*. Bibebook. Accessed December 17, 2022. http://www.bibebook.com/files/ebook/libre/V2/michel_louise_-_memoires_de_louise_michel_ecrits_par_elle-meme.pdf.

Monatte, Pierre. Letter to Leon Trotsky, March 13, 1920. Translated by Mitchell Abidor. Marxists.org. Accessed December 17, 2022. https://www.marxists.org/archive/monatte/1920/letter-trotsky.htm.

———. *Syndicalisme révolutionnaire et communisme, Les archives de Pierre Monatte*. Paris: Éditions Maspero, 1968.

Nadeau, Maurice. *Documents surréalistes*. Paris: Éditions du Seuil, 1948.

Nurnberg, Pascal. "Nestor Makhno et l'Armée insurrectionnelle d'Ukraine." *Le Monde libertaire*, December 9–15, 2010.

Orwell, George. *Homage to Catalonia / Down and Out in Paris and London*. Boston: Houghton Mifflin Harcourt, 2010.

Pannekoek, Anton. "The Proletarian Revolution." In *Lenin as Philosopher*. Accessed December 17, 2022. https://www.marxists.org/archive/pannekoe/1938/lenin/index.htm#n1.

———. *Workers' Councils*. Edited by Robert F. Barsky. Edinburgh: AK Press, 2003.

Paz, Abel. *Buenaventura Durruti: Un combattant libertaire dans la révolution espagnole*. Paris: Éditions de Paris, 2000.

———. *Durruti in the Spanish Revolution*. Translated by Chuck Morse. Chico, CA: AK Press, 2007.

Pereira, Irène. *L'anarchisme dans les textes—Anthologie libertaire*. Paris: Éditions Textuel, 2011.

Péret, Benjamin. *La Commune des Palmares*. Paris: Éditions Syllepse, 1999.

———. *Je ne mange pas de ce pain-là*. Paris: Éditions Syllepse, 2010.

Rancière, Jacques. *Dissenting Words: Interviews with Jacques Rancière*. Edited and translated by Emiliano Battista. London: Bloomsbury Academic, 2017.

———. *Hatred of Democracy*. Translated by Steve Corcoran. New York: Verso Books, 2006.

———. *The Ignorant Schoolmaster: Five Lessons in Intellectual Emancipation*. Translated by Kristin Ross. Stanford: Stanford University Press, 1991.

Roediger, David, and Franklin Rosemont, eds. *Haymarket Scrapbook*. Chicago: Charles H. Kerr Publishing Company, 1986.

Roorda, Henri. *Le pédagogue n'aime pas les enfants*. Paris: Éditions Mille et une nuits, 2012.

Schwarz, Arturo. *Breton/Trotsky*. Paris: Union générale d'éditions, 1977.

Serge, Victor. *Memoirs of a Revolutionary*. Translated by Peter Sedgwick with George Paizis. New York: New York Review Books, 2012.

———. "Thirty Years after the Russian Revolution." In *Russia Twenty Years After*. Edited by Susan Weissman. Atlantic Highlands, NJ: Humanities Press, 1996.

Singer, Daniel. *Prelude to Revolution: France in May 1968*. Chicago: Haymarket Books, 2013.

Skirda, Alexandre. *Kronstadt, 1921: Prolétariat contre bolchévisme*. Paris: Éditions Tête de feuilles, 1971.

Soleno, Wilebaldo. *Le POUM: Révolution dans la guerre d'Espagne*. Paris: Éditions Syllepse, 2002.

Stalin, Joseph. *Works*, vol. 1, *November 1901–April 1907*. Moscow: Foreign Languages Publishing House, 1954. Accessed June 27, 2022. https://www.marxists.org/reference/archive/stalin/works/1906/12/x01.htm.

Stirner, Max. *The Ego and Its Own*. Edited by David Leopold. Cambridge: Cambridge University Press, 1995.

Ternon, Yves. *Makhno: La révolte anarchiste*. Brussels: Éditions Complexe, 1981.

Tiedemann, Rolf. Epilogue to *Charles Baudelaire: Ein Lyriker im Zeitalter des Hochkapitalismus*, by Walter Benjamin. Frankfurt: Suhrkamp Verlag, 1980

———. "Historical Materialism or Political Messianism?" In *Benjamin: Philosophy, History, Aesthetics*, edited by Gary Smith, translated by Barton Byg, Jeremy Gaines, and Doris L. Jones. Chicago: University of Chicago Press, 1983.

Trotsky, Leon. "The Errors in Principle of Syndicalism." *The Militant* 3, no. 7 (February 15, 1930). Accessed December 17, 2022. https://www.marxists.org/archive/trotsky/1931/unions/4-errors.htm.

———. *History of the Russian Revolution*. Translated by Max Eastman. Chicago: Haymarket Books, 2008.

———. "The Lessons of Spain: The Last Warning." *Socialist Appeal* 2, no. 2 (December 1937). Accessed December 17, 2022. https://www.marxists.org/archive/trotsky/1937/xx/spain01.htm.

———. "Stalinism and Bolshevism." Pts. 1 and 2. *Socialist Appeal* 1, no. 7 (September 25, 1937); no. 8 (October 2, 1937). Accessed December 17, 2022. https://www.marxists.org/archive/trotsky/1937/08/stalinism.htm

Index

Page numbers in *italic* refer to illustrations. "Passim" (literally "scattered") indicates intermittent discussion of a topic over a cluster of pages.

Monatte letter to, 51–52;
union militarization, 148
Trotsky, Natalia. *See* Sedova,
Natalia
Trotskyists, 118; Brazil, 37, 72;
France, 30, 33, 72; Spain, 25

Ukraine: Makhno, 100–105
Union des jeunesses
communistes marxistes-
léninistes, 33
Unione Sindacale Italiana. *See*
Italian Syndicalist Union
unions and parties, 146–51
USSR. *See* Soviet Union

Varlin, Eugène, 5
Vie ouvrière, 14
Vivas, Esther: *Planeta Indignado*,
38
La Voix du peuple, 14
Voline, 61, 84, 104, 166n3 (Emma)

Weber, Henri, 30–31
workers' councils, 130, 131, 137,
149; Russia, 84; Spain, 21
Workers' Councils (Pannekoek),
150
Workers' Party of Marxist
Unification (Spain).
See Partido Obrero de
Unificación Marxista
(POUM)
World Social Forum (WSF), 38;
Porto Alegre, 2001, 35, 37
World Trade Organization
protests, Seattle, December
1999, 34
World War I, 50–51, 53, 61, 83;
Treaty of Brest-Litovsk, 83,
101, 167n6

Yarchuk, Efim, 84

Zapata, Emiliano, 75–76
Zapatistas, 34, 75–78, 128–31
passim, 144
Zinoviev, Grigory, 62, 91, 96, 98

About the Authors

Michael Löwy, born in Brazil, has lived in Paris since 1969, and was a member of the Ligue communiste révolutionnaire (French section of the Fourth International) until its dissolution in 2009. His books and articles, including *the Theory of Revolution in Young Marx* (Chicago: Haymarket Books, 2005) and *Franz Kafka: Subversive Dreamer* (Ann Arbor: Michigan University Press, 2016) have been translated into thirty languages. He is emeritus research director of the CNRS (National Center for Scientific Research), Paris.

Olivier Besancenot was born near Paris in 1974 and worked for many years as a mail carrier. In 2002 and 2007 he was the Ligue communiste révolutionnaire candidate in the French presidential elections, getting some 1.5 million votes. He is currently the spokesperson for the New Anticapitalist Party.

Löwy and Besancenot are coauthors of *Che Guevara: His Revolutionary Legacy* (New York, Monthly Review Press, 2009); and *Marx in Paris, 1871: Jenny's "Blue Notebook"* (Chicago: Haymarket, 2022).

About the Translator
David Campbell is a writer, translator, funeral director/embalmer, and former antifascist political prisoner. Originally

from Virginia, he lived in New York City for ten years before moving to Paris in 2021 to pursue a master's in translation at the Sorbonne Nouvelle's École supérieure d'interprètes et de traducteurs. His writing has appeared in Slate, Huffington Post, The Appeal, Truthout, and elsewhere, and his translations have appeared in publications including *Bateau*, *Post(blank)*, and *Barricade*, among others. You can find him on Twitter at @ab_dac.

ABOUT PM PRESS

PM Press is an independent, radical publisher of books and media to educate, entertain, and inspire. Founded in 2007 by a small group of people with decades of publishing, media, and organizing experience, PM Press amplifies the voices of radical authors, artists, and activists.  Our aim is to deliver bold political ideas and vital stories to people from all walks of life and arm the dreamers to demand the impossible. We have sold millions of copies of our books, most often one at a time, face to face. We're old enough to know what we're doing and young enough to know what's at stake. Join us to create a better world.

PM Press
PO Box 23912
Oakland, CA 94623
www.pmpress.org

PM Press in Europe
europe@pmpress.org
www.pmpress.org.uk

FRIENDS OF PM PRESS

These are indisputably momentous times—the
financial system is melting down globally and
the Empire is stumbling. Now more than ever
there is a vital need for radical ideas.

In the many years since its founding—and on
a mere shoestring—PM Press has risen to the formidable challenge
of publishing and distributing knowledge and entertainment for the
struggles ahead. With hundreds of releases to date, we have published
an impressive and stimulating array of literature, art, music, politics, and
culture. Using every available medium, we've succeeded in connecting
those hungry for ideas and information to those putting them into
practice.

Friends of PM allows you to directly help impact, amplify, and revitalize
the discourse and actions of radical writers, filmmakers, and artists. It
provides us with a stable foundation from which we can build upon our
early successes and provides a much-needed subsidy for the materials
that can't necessarily pay their own way. You can help make that
happen—and receive every new title automatically delivered to your
door once a month—by joining as a Friend of PM Press. And, we'll throw
in a free T-shirt when you sign up.

Here are your options:

- **$30 a month** Get all books and pamphlets plus a 50% discount on all
  webstore purchases

- **$40 a month** Get all PM Press releases (including CDs and DVDs)
  plus a 50% discount on all webstore purchases

- **$100 a month** Superstar—Everything plus PM merchandise, free
  downloads, and a 50% discount on all webstore purchases

For those who can't afford $30 or more a month, we have **Sustainer
Rates** at $15, $10 and $5. Sustainers get a free PM Press T-shirt and a
50% discount on all purchases from our website.

Your Visa or Mastercard will be billed once a month, until you tell us to
stop. Or until our efforts succeed in bringing the revolution around. Or
the financial meltdown of Capital makes plastic redundant. Whichever
comes first.

DEPARTMENT OF ANTHROPOLOGY & SOCIAL CHANGE

Anthropology and Social Change, housed within the California Institute of Integral Studies, is a small innovative graduate department with a particular focus on activist scholarship, militant research, and social change. We offer both masters and doctoral degree programs.

Our unique approach to collaborative research methodology dissolves traditional barriers between research and political activism, between insiders and outsiders, and between researchers and protagonists. Activist research is a tool for "creating the conditions we describe." We engage in the process of co-research to explore existing alternatives and possibilities for social change.

Anthropology and Social Change
anth@ciis.edu
1453 Mission Street
94103
San Francisco, California
www.ciis.edu/academics/graduate-programs/anthropology-and-social-change

Critique of the Gotha Program

Karl Marx
with an Introduction by Peter Hudis
and a Foreword by Peter Linebaugh

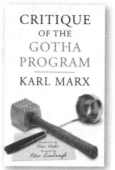

ISBN: 978-1-62963-916-1
$15.95   156 pages

Marx's *Critique of the Gotha Program* is a
revelation. It offers the fullest elaboration of
his vision for a communist future, free from the shackles of capital, but
also the state. Neglected by the statist versions of socialism, whether
Social Democratic or Stalinist that left a wreckage of coercion and
disillusionment in their wake, this new annotated translation of Marx's
Critique makes clear for the first time the full emancipatory scope of
Marx's notion of life after capitalism. An erudite new introduction by
Peter Hudis plumbs the depth of Marx's argument, elucidating how
his vision of communism, and the transition to it, was thoroughly
democratic. At a time when the rule of capital is being questioned
and challenged, this volume makes an essential contribution to a real
alternative to capitalism, rather than piecemeal reforms. In the twenty-
first century, when it has never been more needed, here is Marx at his
most liberatory.

"*This is a compelling moment for a return to Marx's most visionary writings.
Among those is his often neglected,* Critique of the Gotha Program. *In
this exciting new translation, we can hear Marx urging socialists of his day
to remain committed to a truly radical break with capitalism. And in Peter
Hudis's illuminating introductory essay we are reminded that Marx's vision
of a society beyond capitalism was democratic and emancipatory to its very
core. This book is a major addition to the anti-capitalist library.*"
—David McNally, Distinguished Professor of History, University of
Houston and author of *Monsters of the Market*

"*In their penetrating account of Marx's famous hatchet job on the 19th-
century left, Hudis and Anderson go to the heart of issues haunting the left
in the 21st century: what would a society look like without work, wages,
GDP growth, and human self-oppression.*"
—Paul Mason, writer for *New Statesman* and author of *Postcapitalism: A
Guide to Our Future*

Wobblies and Zapatistas: Conversations on Anarchism, Marxism and Radical History

Staughton Lynd and Andrej Grubačić

ISBN: 978-1-60486-041-2
$20.00   300 pages

Wobblies and Zapatistas offers the reader an encounter between two generations and two traditions. Andrej Grubačić is an anarchist from the Balkans. Staughton Lynd is a lifelong pacifist, influenced by Marxism. They meet in dialogue in an effort to bring together the anarchist and Marxist traditions, to discuss the writing of history by those who make it, and to remind us of the idea that "my country is the world." Encompassing a Left libertarian perspective and an emphatically activist standpoint, these conversations are meant to be read in the clubs and affinity groups of the new Movement.

The authors accompany us on a journey through modern revolutions, direct actions, anti-globalist counter summits, Freedom Schools, Zapatista cooperatives, Haymarket and Petrograd, Hanoi and Belgrade, 'intentional' communities, wildcat strikes, early Protestant communities, Native American democratic practices, the Workers' Solidarity Club of Youngstown, occupied factories, self-organized councils and soviets, the lives of forgotten revolutionaries, Quaker meetings, antiwar movements, and prison rebellions. Neglected and forgotten moments of interracial self-activity are brought to light. The book invites the attention of readers who believe that a better world, on the other side of capitalism and state bureaucracy, may indeed be possible.

"There's no doubt that we've lost much of our history. It's also very clear that those in power in this country like it that way. Here's a book that shows us why. It demonstrates not only that another world is possible, but that it already exists, has existed, and shows an endless potential to burst through the artificial walls and divisions that currently imprison us. An exquisite contribution to the literature of human freedom, and coming not a moment too soon."

—David Graeber, author of *Fragments of an Anarchist Anthropology* and *Direct Action: An Ethnography*

Libertarian Socialism: Politics in Black and Red

Edited by Alex Prichard, Ruth Kinna, Saku Pinta, and David Berry

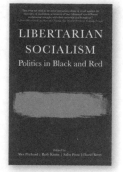

ISBN: 978-1-62963-390-9
$26.95   368 pages

The history of anarchist-Marxist relations is usually told as a history of factionalism and division. These essays, based on original research and written especially for this collection, reveal some of the enduring sores in the revolutionary socialist movement in order to explore the important, too often neglected left-libertarian currents that have thrived in revolutionary socialist movements. By turns, the collection interrogates the theoretical boundaries between Marxism and anarchism and the process of their formation, the overlaps and creative tensions that shaped left-libertarian theory and practice, and the stumbling blocks to movement cooperation. Bringing together specialists working from a range of political perspectives, the book charts a history of radical twentieth-century socialism, and opens new vistas for research in the twenty-first. Contributors examine the political and social thought of a number of leading socialists—Marx, Morris, Sorel, Gramsci, Guérin, C.L.R. James, Hardt and Negri—and key movements including the Situationist International, Socialisme ou Barbarie and Council Communism. Analysis of activism in the UK, Australasia, and the U.S. serves as the prism to discuss syndicalism, carnival anarchism, and the anarchistic currents in the U.S. civil rights movement.

Contributors include Paul Blackledge, Lewis H. Mates, Renzo Llorente, Carl Levy, Christian Høgsbjerg, Andrew Cornell, Benoît Challand, Jean-Christophe Angaut, Toby Boraman, and David Bates.

"Libertarian Socialism: Politics in Black and Red *is an invaluable contribution to historical scholarship and libertarian politics. The collection of essays contained in the book has the great virtue of offering both analytical perspectives on ideas, and historical perspectives on movements. The contributions examine classical themes in anarchist politics such as individual liberty, whilst also exploring more neglected thinkers and themes from a libertarian standpoint, such as C.L.R. James and race. There can be little doubt that the volume will be of major interest to historians, theorists, students and activists.*"
—Darrow Schecter, reader in Italian, School of History, Art History and Philosophy, University of Sussex

For a Libertarian Communism

Daniel Guérin
Edited by David Berry,
translated by Mitchell Abidor

ISBN: 978-1-62963-236-0
$14.95   160 pages

In his foreword to an earlier collection of
essays on libertarian communism, Daniel
Guérin addressed himself to younger people
"alienated from ideologies and 'isms' shorn of
any meaning by an earlier generation" and particularly from "socialism,
which has so often been betrayed by those who claimed to speak in its
name, and which now provokes an understandable skepticism."

In this collection of essays, written between the 1950s and 1980s and
published here for the first time in English, Guérin not only provides a
critique of the socialist and communist parties of his day, he analyzes
some of the most fundamental and pressing questions with which all
radicals must engage. He does this by revisiting and attempting to draw
lessons from the history of the revolutionary movement from the French
Revolution, through the conflicts between anarchists and Marxists
in the International Workingmen's Association and the Russian and
Spanish revolutions, to the social revolution of 1968. These are not just
abstract theoretical reflections, but are informed by the experiences of
a lifetime of revolutionary commitments and by his constant willingness
to challenge orthodoxies of all kinds: "Far from allowing ourselves to sink
into doubt, inaction, and despair, the time has come for the left to begin
again from zero, to rethink its problems from their very foundations. The
failure of both reformism and Stalinism imposes on us the urgent duty
to find a way of reconciling (proletarian) democracy with socialism,
freedom with Revolution."

*"Over six decades Daniel Guérin had a record of willingness to cooperate
with any section of the French left that shared his fundamental goals of
proletarian self-emancipation, colonial liberation, and sexual freedom. He
was a vigorous polemicist but saw no fragment of the left, however obscure,
as beneath his attention. He was also typically generous, never seeking to
malign his opponents, however profoundly he disagreed with them. He was
always willing to challenge orthodoxy, whether Marxist or anarchist. Yet
behind the varying formulations one consistent principle remained: 'The
Revolution of our age will be made from below—or not at all.'"*
—Ian Birchall, author of *The Spectre of Babeuf*, *Sartre Against Stalinism*,
and *A Rebel's Guide to Lenin*

Politics at a Distance from the State: Radical and African Perspectives

Kirk Helliker and Lucien van der Walt with a Preface by John Holloway

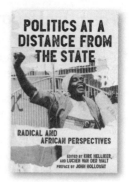

ISBN: 978-1-62963-943-7
$19.95   192 pages

For decades, most anti-capitalist and anti-imperialist movements identified radical change with capturing state power. The collapse of statist projects from the 1970s fostered both neo-liberalism and a global crisis of left and working-class politics. But it also opened space for rediscovering democratic, society-centered, and anti-capitalist modes of bottom-up change, operating at a distance from the state. This resurgent alternative has influenced the Zapatistas in Mexico, Rojava in Syria, Occupy, and independent unions and struggles worldwide around austerity, land, and the city. Its lineages include anarchism, syndicalism, autonomist Marxism, philosophers like Alain Badiou, and popular praxis.

This pathbreaking volume helps recover this once sidelined politics, with a focus on South Africa and Zimbabwe. It includes a dossier of texts from a century of anarchists, syndicalists, radical unionists, and anti-apartheid activists in South Africa. Originating in an African summit of scholars, social movements, and anti-apartheid veterans, this book also features a preface from John Holloway.

"Yes, universities may produce assemblies which serve the people. So, in 2012 at Grahamstown, South Africa, did Rhodes University (despite the name), and in that service produced a people's knowledge to transform the economic, material, social, family, political, educational, and spiritual institutions of capitalism at their core, without hierarchy, racism, oppression, or chauvinism of any kind. With sober care, practical acumen, and passionate eloquence the knowledge from that assembly is presented here. Absorb this knowledge and sense the future!"
—Peter Linebaugh, coauthor of The Many-Headed Hydra: Sailors, Slaves, Commoners and the Hidden History of the Revolutionary Atlantic (with Marcus Rediker)

From K from PM Press

KAIROS

Mutual Aid: An Illuminated Factor of Evolution

Peter Kropotkin
Illustrated by N.O. Bonzo with an
Introduction by David Graeber &
Andrej Grubačić, Foreword by Ruth
Kinna, Postscript by GATS, and an
Afterword by Allan Antliff

ISBN: 978-1-62963-874-4 (paperback)
        978-1-62963-875-1 (hardcover)
$30.00/$59.95   336 pages

One hundred years after his death, Peter Kropotkin is still one of
the most inspirational figures of the anarchist movement. It is often
forgotten that Kropotkin was also a world-renowned geographer whose
seminal critique of the hypothesis of competition promoted by social
Darwinism helped revolutionize modern evolutionary theory. An admirer
of Darwin, he used his observations of life in Siberia as the basis for his
1902 collection of essays *Mutual Aid: A Factor of Evolution*. Kropotkin
demonstrated that mutually beneficial cooperation and reciprocity—in
both individuals and as a species—plays a far more important role
in the animal kingdom and human societies than does individualized
competitive struggle. Kropotkin carefully crafted his theory making the
science accessible. His account of nature rejected Rousseau's romantic
depictions and ethical socialist ideas that cooperation was motivated
by the notion of "universal love." His understanding of the dynamics of
social evolution shows us the power of cooperation—whether it is bison
defending themselves against a predator or workers unionizing against
their boss. His message is clear: solidarity is strength!

Every page of this new edition of *Mutual Aid* has been beautifully
illustrated by one of anarchism's most celebrated current artists, N.O.
Bonzo. The reader will also enjoy original artwork by GATS and insightful
commentary by David Graeber, Ruth Kinna, Andrej Grubačić, and Allan
Antliff.

*"N.O. Bonzo has created a rare document, updating Kropotkin's anarchist
classic* Mutual Aid, *by intertwining compelling imagery with an updated
text. Filled with illustrious examples, their art gives the words and histories,
past and present, resonance for new generations to seed flowers of
cooperation to push through the concrete of resistance to show liberatory
possibilities for collective futures."*
—scott crow, author of *Black Flags and Windmills* and *Setting Sights*

KAIROS

Re-enchanting the World: Feminism and the Politics of the Commons

Silvia Federici
with a Foreword by Peter Linebaugh

ISBN: 978-1-62963-569-9
$19.95   240 pages

Silvia Federici is one of the most important contemporary theorists of capitalism and feminist movements. In this collection of her work spanning over twenty years, she provides a detailed history and critique of the politics of the commons from a feminist perspective. In her clear and combative voice, Federici provides readers with an analysis of some of the key issues and debates in contemporary thinking on this subject.

Drawing on rich historical research, she maps the connections between the previous forms of enclosure that occurred with the birth of capitalism and the destruction of the commons and the "new enclosures" at the heart of the present phase of global capitalist accumulation. Considering the commons from a feminist perspective, this collection centers on women and reproductive work as crucial to both our economic survival and the construction of a world free from the hierarchies and divisions capital has planted in the body of the world proletariat. Federici is clear that the commons should not be understood as happy islands in a sea of exploitative relations but rather autonomous spaces from which to challenge the existing capitalist organization of life and labor.

"Silvia Federici's theoretical capacity to articulate the plurality that fuels the contemporary movement of women in struggle provides a true toolbox for building bridges between different features and different people."
—Massimo De Angelis, professor of political economy, University of East London

"Silvia Federici's work embodies an energy that urges us to rejuvenate struggles against all types of exploitation and, precisely for that reason, her work produces a common: a common sense of the dissidence that creates a community in struggle."
—Maria Mies, coauthor of *Ecofeminism*

From **K** from PM Press

Between Thought and Expression Lies a Lifetime: Why Ideas Matter

James Kelman & Noam Chomsky

ISBN: 978-1-62963-880-5 (paperback)
      978-1-62963-886-7 (hardcover)
$19.95/$39.95   304 pages

"The world is full of information. What do we do when we get the information, when we have digested the information, what do we do then? Is there a point where ye say, yes, stop, now I shall move on."

This exhilarating collection of essays, interviews, and correspondence—spanning the years 1988 through 2018, and reaching back a decade more—is about the simple concept that ideas matter. They mutate, inform, create fuel for thought, and inspire actions.

As Kelman says, the State relies on our suffocation, that we cannot hope to learn "the truth. But whether we can or not is beside the point. We must grasp the nettle, we assume control and go forward."

Between Thought and Expression Lies a Lifetime is an impassioned, elucidating, and often humorous collaboration. Philosophical and intimate, it is a call to ponder, imagine, explore, and act.

"The real reason Kelman, despite his stature and reputation, remains something of a literary outsider is not, I suspect, so much that great, radical Modernist writers aren't supposed to come from working-class Glasgow, as that great, radical Modernist writers are supposed to be dead. Dead, and wrapped up in a Penguin Classic: that's when it's safe to regret that their work was underappreciated or misunderstood (or how little they were paid) in their lifetimes. You can write what you like about Beckett or Kafka and know they're not going to come round and tell you you're talking nonsense, or confound your expectations with a new work. Kelman is still alive, still writing great books, climbing."
—James Meek, *London Review of Books*

"A true original . . . A real artist. . . . It's now very difficult to see which of his peers can seriously be ranked alongside [Kelman] without ironic eyebrows being raised."
—Irvine Welsh, *Guardian*

From K from PM Press

KAIROS

Archive That, Comrade! Left Legacies and the Counter Culture of Remembrance

Phil Cohen

ISBN: 978-1-62963-506-4
$19.95   160 pages

Archive That, Comrade! explores issues of archival theory and practice that arise for any project aspiring to provide an open-access platform for political dialogue and democratic debate. It is informed by the author's experience of writing a memoir about his involvement in the London underground scene of the 1960s, the London street commune movement, and the occupation of 144 Piccadilly, an event that hit the world's headlines for ten days in July 1969.

After a brief introduction that sets the contemporary scene of 'archive fever,' the book considers what the political legacy of 1960s counter culture reveals about the process of commemoration. The argument then opens out to discuss the notion of historical legacy and its role in the 'dialectic of generations'. How far can the archive serve as a platform for dialogue and debate between different generations of activists in a culture that fetishises the evanescent present, practices a profound amnesia about its past, and forecloses the sociological imagination of an alternative future? The following section looks at the emergence of a complex apparatus of public fame and celebrity around the spectacle of dissidence and considers whether the Left has subverted or merely mirrored the dominant forms of reputation-making and public recognition. Can the Left establish its own autonomous model of commemoration?

The final section takes up the challenge of outlining a model for the democratic archive as a revisionary project, creating a resource for building collective capacity to sustain struggles of long duration. A postscript examines how archival strategies of the alt-right have intervened at this juncture to elaborate a politics of false memory.

"Has the Left got a past? And if so, is that past best forgotten? Who was it who said, 'Let the dead bury their dead'? Phil Cohen's book is a searing meditation on the politics of memory, written by someone for whom 'the '60s' are still alive—and therefore horrible, unfinished, unforgivable, tremendous, undead. His book brings back to life the William Faulkner cliché. The past for Cohen is neither dead nor alive. It's not even past, more's the pity."
—T.J. Clark, author of *The Sight of Death*